LIVE FROM

WORLD WAR II

This book is dedicated to Lt. Marvin Lazette, and the millions of soldiers like him who risked and sacrificed their lives so that I would have the freedom to write this book.

Preface

In 1940, the United States of America was a nation at peace. The country watched the advancement of war in Europe with a wary eye while it debated what action should be taken. The nation was sorely divided on what its involvement should be. This debate raged among not only the citizenry, but was also played out in the public sparring between aviation hero Charles Lindbergh and President Franklin D. Roosevelt. Lindbergh, a colonel in the air force had traveled to Germany often and toured their aviation factories and facilities. His findings were presented to congress where he testified that the United States was far behind the Germans in the development of war time aircraft. Because of this he concluded that the United States should begin negotiating a neutrality pact with Germany. Ironically, it was Lindbergh's father, Congressmen Charles August Lindbergh, who led the movement to keep the Unites States out of World War One.

Lindbergh soon became the spokesman for the antiwar "America First Committee". He was one part hero and one part charismatic which made him perfect for the role. He would speak to overflowing crowds at sites such as Madison Square Garden in New York and Soldier Field in Chicago and he was met by enthusiastic throngs who seemed attentive to his message and were willing to listen to his pacifistic thoughts and opinions.

Meanwhile, President Roosevelt had a firm conviction to assist Europe by any means against the German aggression, and compared Lindbergh to United States Representative Clement Vallandingam. Vallandingham was the leader of the Copperhead Movement during the Civil War (Copperheads were residents of the north who were against the war with the South). Lindbergh subsequently resigned his commission in the Air Corps in response to Roosevelt's public attack questioning his loyalty saying "he could find no honorable alternative". But that didn't stop Lindbergh from continuing to wage his war against war. He continued to make stops anywhere people would listen to his plea to avoid war at any cost. President Roosevelt was convinced Lindbergh was a Nazi after listening to his continued attacks against United States involvement in Europe.

Against the backdrop of this very public debate and the many private discussions that were waged in every home in America, and while the nation listened as two of its greatest public figures tried to convince the nation which direction was best, events were happening that would determine the nation's course of action. Takeo Yoshikawa, a Japanese spy, arrived in Honolulu to begin studying the fleet at Pearl Harbor.

The United States had no plans to enter the war in Europe, however, Greenville Clark, chairman of the American Bar Association, led the initiative to pass the Selective Training and Service Act of 1940, also known as the Burke-Wadsworth Act. This was the first peacetime draft in the history of the United States and was created soon after Germany invaded Poland which forced Britain and France to declare war on Germany. It initially required civilian males between the ages of 21 and 30 to register with their local draft board. Each draft board was given a recruitment quota and complete discretion on how that quota was to be met. The draft board in Monroe, Michigan was no exception to the quota rule.

Monroe was founded by French missionaries in 1785 making it one of the oldest cities in Michigan. The French found Monroe's location ideal for trading and commerce being adjacent to Lake Erie and on the Raisin River. Monroe continued to thrive long after the end of fur trading and birch bark canoes. It soon found itself in close proximity to a man named Henry Ford and the automobile industry he launched. Now, instead of trading posts, there were factories creating jobs that touched the lives of nearly every resident of Monroe.

Marvin Lazette was a twenty five year old factory worker and he helped Monroe make its recruitment goal in April of 1941. Marvin was one of the older men on the bus of enlistees pulling out of the bus depot and heading to Fort Knox. He was only interested in completing his enlistment obligation, returning to his job at the factory, marrying his girlfriend Bertha Balk, and raising a family. He promised her he would write as often as possible during his one year enlistment.

His one year became four, and these are his letters home.

Live from

World War II

By Lt. Marvin Lazette

Compiled and Annotated by Alan Lazette

APRIL 20 1941

"We rode all day Thursday and got as far as Indianapolis, Indiana. Just as we pulled in about dark it started to rain. We had to pitch tents in the pouring rain and ankle deep mud. Then on top of this the water got too deep so we had to huddle in the trucks. We had to get up early, about 3:00 so we didn't wash or take our clothes off for 2 days. What a life!"

APRIL 24, 1941

"I see Greenberg will be in the good old army"

If you are living in the vicinity of Detroit, you are destined to become a Detroit Tiger fan. Such notable legends such as Ty Cobb, Mickey Cochrane, Charlie Gehringer, and of course Hank Greenberg insured your induction into the Detroit Tiger family.

Henry "Hank" Greenberg was the first Jewish superstar in American professional sports. He attracted national attention when he refused to play baseball on Yom Kippur. He was the youngest player in the majors when he began playing at the age of 19 and became the first player to earn $80,000 when he was sold to the Pittsburgh Pirates in 1947. Greenberg was named to the All Star team five times and was the American League's most valuable player twice. He was elected into the hall of fame in 1956 and holds the American League record for most RBI's in a single season by a right handed batter and only left hand hitting Lou Gehrig has more.

Greenberg was initially classified as 4F (he was declined for flat feet) and rumors circulated that he had bribed the recruitment board. He was concerned that he would be compared to heavy weight boxer Jack Dempsey who was defiled for his failure to serve in World War One. Greenberg asked to be examined again and was found fit to serve. Upon being drafted his salary was cut from $55,000 a year to $21.00 a month. Greenberg was not bitter stating "I made up my mind to go when I was called. My country comes first." Ironically, Greenberg was released from service due to age just two days before the Japanese bombing of Pearl Harbor. Greenberg enlisted again when the United States entered World War Two, becoming the first major league player to do so. He was commissioned as a first lieutenant in the United States Air Force and served forty five months, the longest of any major league player. He served mainly in the China-Burma-India theatre scouting locations for B-29 bases.

Hank Greenberg wasn't alone in his dedication to serve his country. He was joined by five hundred other baseball players, eighty members of the National Hockey League joined the Canadian or United States military, and six hundred players from the National Football League all served in World War Two.

APRIL 26, 1941

"We will be leaving Ft. Knox soon and will be on maneuvers for the summer and I don't see how you will be able to find us"

Fort Knox was named after Henry Knox, the continental army's chief of artillery during the revolutionary war and the country's first Secretary of War. It was first constructed to stop an anticipated British invasion prior to the Civil War. During the Civil War, both Union and Confederate troops occupied the territory upon which the fort was constructed. Its most celebrated graduate is General George Patton.

"I sort of wonder if Pat will remember me when I get a chance to get back"

At his point, Marvin was only concerned with his one year enlistment and the thought of four years away from home had never entered his mind. Pat, born in 1937, was Marvin's sister and the youngest in the family. A total of twenty one years separated Marvin from Pat and those years were filled with five other sisters and one brother. Marvin's older brother Clayton was not eligible for the draft due to a breathing disorder. By the time the war had ended, three of Marvin's family had married three from his girlfriend Bertha's family. The three intermarriages made for some very interesting family reunions.

APRIL 28, 1941

The first week at Fort Knox consisted of days filled with training and work assignments. Marvin soon learned the reason it was called "basic training". Hours of travel in the back of trucks, digging fox holes, rigging tents, and twenty four hour guard duty became a way of life. Still, he knew that for him to receive letters, he would have to write letters home. He had to use every possible empty minute to write another letter home.

"I had guard duty starting at 11:30 Saturday morning and ending at 4:30 Sunday afternoon. Boy am I tired with no sleep for about 30 hours."

MAY 9, 1941

Marvin and some fellow enlistees took advantage of a long weekend away from the army with a trip to see the nearby sights.

"We arrived at Mammouth Cave on Thursday afternoon. The cave was really worth the dollar we paid for admission."

"I didn't get to the Kentucky Derby but I did see Whirlaway and some of the other horses in practice."

Anyone who had the opportunity to see Whirlaway run experienced the thrill of their lifetime. There was never a horse that overcame such a huge handicap and had the success that Whirlaway achieved. Whirlaway was the winner of the Triple Crown in 1941 and was named Horse of the Year. However, early in his career, both his owner and trainer wondered if the horse would ever win a race. Whirlaway had a tendency to drift to the middle of the track during a race and become trapped among the other horses. Time and time again the horse would be in position to win, only to drift and finish back among the pack. Finally, trainer Ben Jones outfitted the horse with a full cup blinker over its right eye with a slit that allowed the horse a tiny field of vision. This stroke of genius enabled the horse to win every race for the remainder of its career.

MAY 26, 1941

"I walked all around the camp and finally ended up at the show. For 20 cents I saw a double feature "Blondie Goes Latin" and "Dead Men Talk" with Charlie Chan."

There were a total of twenty eight Blondie films produced from 1938 until 1950 and Penny Singleton starred as Blondie in every one of them. That is two Blondie movies per year. In addition to the movies, she also portrayed Blondie on the radio series from 1938 until 1950. Penny Singleton became the first woman president of the AFL-CIO. She ended her career as the voice of Jane Jetson.

MAY 29, 1941

The fireside chat became the best way for President
Roosevelt to inform the American public of his thoughts
and concerns. Every address was enormously successful
and attracted more listeners than most popular radio
shows. Marvin and his fellow barracks mates joined the
rest of the nation listening to Roosevelt's "Proclamation of
Unlimited National Emergency" speech.

*"By Roosevelt's speech, we may be in more than a
year or may not. It all depends on the conditions next
fall or spring. I don't believe however that we'll stay
much over a year if we do."*

The speech detailed to the American public a state of
"unlimited national emergency" in response to Nazi
Germany's threats of world domination. Roosevelt
explained that the United States is prepared to go to war if
an attack is made on any country vital to our defense. This
was his motivation to rally the isolationists behind his
cause. He stated that bombs dropped on Canada were
just as menacing as ones dropped on the United States
and that we must be prepared to do whatever necessary
to defend our allies at all costs. He specifically warned
Germany that the United States was prepared for war and

concluded with the remark he made famous in his 1933 "Great Depression" speech, "the only thing we have to fear is fear itself."

Free enterprise is alive and well everywhere, even in the army.

"The three of us are starting a haircut business on our own time. We've bought quite a lot of tonics and combs and have about five dollars in our treasury. As soon as we get clippers we will do more business. Woodall Company (Marvin's employer in Monroe) sent us an ironing board and electric steam ironer so we're renting it out depending on how much the person has to iron. It's an easy way to pick up a little extra money."

"I see where the army took over an airplane factory in California. That's the thing to do and not monkey around with these strikers."

While union sentiment was high in the United States, most Americans were outraged about the strike and agreed with Marvin's point of view. . This was especially true with the threat of war growing every day in Europe. Even though the United States was not at war, military goods manufactured in American factories were being shipped to England. In addition, the United States army and navy were gearing up for a possible entry into the war. The strike took place at the North American Aviation Company in Inglewood, California. President Roosevelt thought the strike was "inspired and directed by Communist forces, not interested in the advancement of labor but in the defeat and overthrow of the United States." He then ordered federal troops to seize and safeguard the factory. Although the plant was seized by the government, it was a victory for the union and its strikers as the war department proceeded to operate the plant in accordance with the union's wishes. However, the government of the United States had sent a message to all working men and women regarding how it felt regarding work stoppages in factories it deemed of national interest and security.

JUNE 18, 1941

Remember the haircutting business? Well, it has expanded into the financial industry.

"There are three of us cutting hair and about eight of us from Monroe with an interest in the iron. I collect two bits for a haircut and twenty cents for a guy to press his pants and shirt. We also make a little lending out money as we charge 35 cents on the dollar."

Just to put this lending practice in perspective, the highest allowed lending rate in the United States is 21% in the state of Indiana. This was 150% above that rate!

"I'm writing this while listening to the Louis-Conn fight. It's in the 7th round and I won 50 cents by betting the fight would go 6 rounds and over."

The Joe Louis/Billy Conn fight was watched by a crowd of over 54,000 people crammed into the Polo Grounds, many of whom thought Billy Conn had a chance to defeat the defending heavy weight champion. Conn was attempting to become the first World Light Heavyweight champion in boxing history to win the World Heavyweight championship. Not only that, but he planned to do so without gaining any additional weight for the fight! The fight lasted thirteen rounds and is considered one of the greatest fights in boxing history. As the fight entered round thirteen, many scorecards had Conn ahead in points. It was then that Billy Conn made a decision that he would regret for the rest of his life. Conn decided to try and knock out the defending heavyweight champion as he started the fourteenth round. Joe Louis, knocked out Conn, seizing the moment and cementing his legacy as the greatest heavyweight boxer of all time. Louis, who was only six minutes and two seconds away from losing his crown, instead won a decisive victory over the feisty Billy Conn.

"Yesterday we got our first taste of the actual horrors of war. We went through the gas chamber filled with tear gas. We went through first with gas masks on and it wasn't bad except that your throat and arms really burned something terrible. The second time we went through, we walked in with our masks off. Boy, that gas hit your eyes like someone hitting you in the face with a club. We had to hurry and don our masks and walk around and then take our masks off and dash out in the open air. It really was something as about everyone was crying."

The use of poison gas in World War Two was a very real fear. Poison gas had been used in World War One and many expected it would be used again. As a result, gas mask drills such as the one just described by Marvin became routine. Mustard gas had been used in World War One and blistered the skin causing extreme pain. It was also capable of soaking through most material.

Far more deadly than mustard gas were cyanide, carbon monoxide, and cyanogens chloride. All of these impeded the ability of the blood to absorb oxygen which caused the body to shut down quickly. Death was rapid and painless.

Many variations of nerve gas were available for use in World War Two. Nerve gases attacked the nervous system causing nausea, vomiting, muscular twitching, convulsions, cessation of breathing, and death. Soman was the most deadly of the nerve gases causing victims to go into convulsions a mere seconds after inhalation. According to the United States Army, victims would be dead within two minutes of Soman exposure.

It was estimated that the Germans had stockpiled enough nerve gas to kill the occupants of thirty cities the size of Paris. So, why was nerve gas never used in World War Two? The fear of retaliation and that the enemy may have developed a more virulent poison gas was the main reason. So, in a war where atomic weapons, napalm, unrestricted submarine warfare, and civilians were seen as legitimate targets, no one was willing to risk using a weapon that had become so feared in World War One.

JULY 6, 1941

"I've heard a few of us are to be made PFC's after this month. A PFC gets $38.00 per month and my specialist rating ought to bring my pay well into the forty dollars(around $45.00)."

To put this into perspective, the minimum wage at the time was thirty cents per hour. Milk cost thirty four cents for a gallon and bread was eight cents for a loaf. The average annual salary was just over two thousand dollars.

JULY 7, 1941

"We went over to East St. Louis across the Mississippi River and stayed there until 3 A.M. We couldn't get a place to sleep any place so we finally ended up with 4 of us sleeping on the front lawn of a school. I slept in the car and was rudely awakened by a bunch of kids standing over us shooting cap guns. A woman nearby asked us if we cared for a cup of coffee and we all made a dive for the door. She let us shave and clean up and she had bacon sliced and a bowl of eggs and coffee ready for us. She told us to cook our breakfasts and she bought a couple of Sunday papers for us and jam and rolls. She sat out on the front porch and we had the run of the house. She really was swell to us. Her husband was working at a chemical plant doing defense work and it isn't very many women who would let five soldiers in the house when she was alone."

Fast forward to current time and imagine how this same scene would have played out. Our soldiers probably would have been too terrified to sleep outside and one can only guess about the outcome if they had. And what about a woman, alone in her house, inviting men she doesn't know into her home and cook them breakfast!

"They're having quite an argument about keeping us longer than a year. I suppose Hank and Gabby are glad to know now that they are all set to serve their country."

The argument was based on President Roosevelt's message to congress in which he advised:

"In the absence of further action by the Congress, all of those involved must be released from active service on the expiration date of twelve months. This means that beginning this autumn about two thirds of the army of the United States will begin a demobilization."

President Roosevelt went on to suggest:

"It is therefore obvious that if two thirds of our present army return to civilian life, it will be almost a year before the effective army strength again reaches one million men."

This issue was extremely important to President Roosevelt. So important, that in just a few months his actions will cause heartbreak for many men.

"Frank McHugh and Marjorie Weaver are here with the USO show."

Since 1941, the USO has worked in partnership with the Department of Defense relying heavily on private contributions and on funds, goods, and services from various corporate and individual donors. Although congressionally chartered, it is not a government agency. The USO currently operates 160 centers around the world.

During World War Two the USO became the "home away from home" for many GI's and began a tradition of entertaining the troops.

Frank Mchugh debuted on Broadway in 1925 and Warner Brothers studio hired him in 1930. McHugh played everything from lead actor to sidekick and would often provide comedy relief. He appeared in over 150 films and television productions and worked with almost every star at Warner Brothers. He was a close friend of James Cagney and appeared in more Cagney movies than any other actor.

Marjorie Weaver began her acting career as a stage actress in the early 1930's and also worked as a model and singer. She received her first film role in 1934. From 1938 through 1945 she had twenty seven starring roles. Her most notable film was "Young Mr. Lincoln" in 1939 which starred Henry Fonda.

AUGUST 4, 1941

"Well it looks like you had better give me up for loss and start hunting for a new boyfriend. According to the paper they want to keep us in the army for 2 1/2 years. That will really cause a lot of cussing by me and all the rest if it passes. However, they may pass this to insure our staying until the emergency is over."

The failure of Roosevelt to embroil the country any deeper in the European or the Pacific wars led to a long season of plodding and stumbling on the home front, much of it communicated to the conscript army, which looked only forward to the termination of their year of service. Panic again swept the interventionists, and a new drive to extend the draft built up in the summer of 1941. The most visible of those arguing for this cause was Chief of Staff, General Marshall, who appeared before Congress numerous times to testify of the need to keep draftees beyond their stipulated period of service.

The mood in the army camps grew tense and threats of mass desertion proliferated the country. The ominous acronym "OHIO" (Over the Hill In October) began to appear on barracks walls. A serious crisis was in full bloom by the time a pressure wracked House of Representatives voted on August 12 to extend the period of service. The proposal passed by a lone vote, 203 − 202. The Senate approved the legislation by a wider margin and Roosevelt signed the bill into law on August 18.

But for one vote, every enlisted man saw their one year requirement vanish!

AUGUST 17, 1941

"Don't get the idea that I'm against marriage as I'm not, but you have to go into it with your eyes open. If I get out of this with two arms and two legs, then I'll think seriously about marrying a nice brown eyed girl."

AUGUST 20, 1941

"I think that the allies are opening up at last according to the radio they are blasting France and preparing for a 2^d front very soon. I wish I could be with the marines as they are seeing action and plenty."

On August 15, Robert Stanford Tuck led the first air mission by fighters based in eastern England against enemy occupied territories in France in a "rhubarb" sweep for ground targets. Rhubarb operations were sections of fighters and/or bombers that would take advantage of low cloud and poor visibility. Crossing the English Channel, they would drop below cloud level and search for opportunity targets such as railways, aircraft on the ground, and enemy troops.

AUGUST 22, 1941

"According to the War Department, we may get out in 14 to 16 months. I sure hope everything has quieted down a little by then so I can be home by next fall."

NOVEMBER 12, 1941

"We stayed in tents while we were in St Louis and it was sure cold in the early mornings. I've never seen so many people come to see a parade in my life. They were in trees, windows, roof tops, fire escapes, everywhere."

The St. Louis Globe Democrat headline on November 12 endorsed Marvin's observation:

"Over 300,000 Jam Downtown Streets to See Armistace Parade, Biggest Ever Held Here."

The paper stated over 8000 men and 350 officers from Fort Leonard Wood led the 16,000 marchers through flag draped streets. Aerial bombs signaled the beginning and the milling masses at the starting point began their friendly battle with the law. It took the high prancing horses and fast darting motorcycles of the police to cut a swath for the first infantry to lead the parade. Paper showers from office buildings fell on the marching men and on spectators who lined the curbs twenty deep in some places. At some points, the crowd caused a delay in the parade and reinforcements had to be summoned to clear a path for the parade to continue.

It was a clear indication that the American population was in strong support of their armed forces at a time when the drums of war were beating louder with every passing day. While America had yet to enter the war officially, its support of Europe and its continued emphasis on growing the military made every citizen acutely proud of their country and their military.

NOVEMBER 15, 1941

"I've got a hunch that I will be getting out soon after my year is up, either in May or June."

This would turn out to be a very bad hunch!

"Well dear, I'm starting this letter in a very poor state of mind. I'm really disgusted with this damn army. Today they called all of the 6ᵗʰ Division (of which we are a part of) but only the infantry are going to go to the coal strike area in Pennsylvania. I guess they're expecting trouble there and are sending quite a few troops from here. It hasn't been officially announced as they're trying to keep it quiet but they leave tomorrow morning."

In an effort to keep wages in line, the NWLB (National War Labor Board) came up with a policy known as the "Little Steel Formula." First applied to the steel industry and then to a wide range of corporations, the formula allowed wage increases only at levels that would not increase inflation. Unions argued that the application of this formula crippled collective bargaining and that wage increases were constantly lagging behind inflation. This cycle kept the workers poor and allowed corporations to make huge profits according to the unionists.

As it became clear that the Allies were turning the tide of the war, many unions began to question the wisdom of giving up their right to strike and turning their fate over to a government agency (NWLB) that they could not influence. Although the leaderships of the AFL and CIO stood by their "No Strike Pledge", the President of the United Mine Workers, John L. Lewis, became increasingly vocal in his criticism of this policy. It was universally acknowledged that the coal miners had the dirtiest and most dangerous jobs in America. In addition, most everyone also recognized that the miners were undercompensated for their work. Deciding that the wartime emergency was the perfect opportunity to rectify this imbalance, Lewis led his miners out on strike.

The defiance by Lewis was not surprising. He had made a career of challenging the status quo and he was no great fan of President Roosevelt. Though President Roosevelt was popular among workers, Lewis convinced them that Roosevelt wasn't enough of a friend to them. Lewis went on to state that while Hitler and the Japanese were loathesome, they were no threat to the United States. "While Europe was on the brink of disaster, it must be our care that she does not drag us into the abyss after her."

DECEMBER 8, 1941

"I can't believe the Japs are that despicable. I don't want to fight, but, I will do anything to make sure the world is safe for you. I will go overseas and fight them now to protect Patty and Bobby. I don't think the war will last very long and I will do everything I can to end it as soon as possible."

The attack on Pearl Harbor was 110 minutes that changed the lives of every American citizen, young and old. As the last Japanese plane left Pearl Harbor to return, it left behind over 2,400 dead and 1,200 wounded. And while the attack itself lasted a short time, the planning took months.

Admiral Isoroku Yamamoto devised the plan in January of 1941 and Commander Minoru Genda was the chief architect. The idea was to attack on Sunday in hopes the Americans would be more relaxed and less alert on that day. The Japanese hoped to sink America's air craft carriers, but all three were out to sea, leaving just destroyers for targets. All eight destroyers were either sunk or damaged in the attack, yet six were able to be repaired and see active duty in the war.

In addition to the navy losses, the Japanese targeted airfields at Hickam Field, Wheeler Field, Bellows Field, Shoeefield, and Kaneohe. The planes were lined up wing tip to wing tip to ease in guarding against sabotage. Unfortunately, they made easy targets for the Japanese air force.

The attack was to commence after Japan had informed the United States that is was withdrawing from further peace negotiations. However, the transcription of the message from Japan to its ambassador took too long for the ambassador to deliver it in time to the President. England declared war on Japan nine hours before the United States did to keep Winston Churchill's promise to declare war "within the hour" of a Japanese attack on the United States.

The declaration of war was presented to a joint session of congress as part of Roosevelt's famous "Infamy" speech at 12:30. The Senate passed the declaration of war by a vote of 82-0 at 1:10. The House of Representatives passed the declaration 388-1 with Jeanette Rankin, the first woman elected to congress as the lone dissenter. She declared that "As a woman I can't go to war and I refuse to send anyone else." So incensed at her vote, an angry mob followed her and she was forced to hide in a telephone booth and call the police to rescue her.

DECEMBER 14, 1941

"I know you want to get married and that's the one thing in life that I care about so if you don't want to wait until I get out, I'll buy a ring and marry you the first time I get home. I know you don't like the idea but it shows that I'd do it if you wanted to. I know you want a church wedding, but I'll take you under any circumstances. This may sound like I'm taking a lot for granted but you can save this letter as a proposal. There's another good angle because if we were married and I'd get bumped off, you'd get a pension for life. That's the only way I'd quit loving you anyway is to get a few bullets in or near my heart."

The wedding ultimately took place after the end of the war, in December of 1945.

DECEMBER 22,1941

"Just remember there are thousands worse off than we are like the English kids over there and all over separated from their mothers and fathers."

The evacuation of civilians in Britain during the World War Two was designed particularly to save the children from the risk of aerial bombing of urban areas by moving them to areas thought to be less at risk. Operation Pied Piper began on September 1, 1939 (two days before the declaration of war) and officially relocated more than 3.5 million children and adults. Further waves of evacuations occurred from the south and east coasts when seaborne invasions were expected. Some evacuation areas became overwhelmed causing school and family groups to become separated as they transferred from mainline trains to local transport.

In the first three days of the official evacuation, a total of 1.5 million people were moved. These included over 1.3 million mothers and children, 13,000 pregnant women, 7,000 disabled persons, and over 100,000 teachers. An additional 2 million wealthy individuals evacuated privately into rural hotels, Canada, or the United States. After the fall of France in 1940, an additional 300,000 children were moved as a possible invasion appeared more plausible.

It was important to safeguard the assets of the country as well. Art treasures were sent to distant storage facilities, the Bank of England moved to the small town of Overton, and over 2 thousand tons of gold was shipped to the Bank of Canada in Ottawa. Most major corporations relocated their headquarters and/or their vital records.

Government functions, services, and dignitaries were also relocated. Under "Plan Yellow", over 20 thousand civil servants and their paperwork were sent to available hotels. Other hotels were requisitioned by the government and emptied for possible last ditch moves should London be destroyed or threatened by invasion. Under this plan, even Winston Churchill and King George VI had pre planned locations waiting for them.

DECEMBER 26, 1941

"I was afraid you wouldn't be there as I put the call in about 3:30 and they said it would take about 4 hours before I would get through. I guess the lines

were really jammed. Ted Oberlieter called at 7:00 p.m. and waited until 11:00 p.m."

JANUARY 1, 1942

"This camp has had over 200 guys go over the hill since before Xmas and they have over 600 in the different guard houses. It's easy to understand when they take furloughs away and then make you work on holidays."

"Some guys came over and got me to go to town with them to eat supper and go to a show. "They Died with Their Boots On was on and I razzed these guys about Monroe being such a famous city".

The movie was an account of the life of General George Armstrong Custer and his famous battle at the Little Big Horn. It starred Errol Flynn as General Custer and Olivia de Havilland as his wife Elizabeth Bacon Custer. Custer was admitted to the West Point Academy in 1858 where he graduated last in his class. However, with the outbreak of the Civil War, all potential officers were needed and Custer was called to serve with the Union Army. He developed a strong reputation during the Civil War and fought his initial engagement in the first Battle of Bull Run. Custer's association with several important officers and his success as a highly effective cavalry commander helped his career and he was promoted to Major General. At the conclusion of the Appomattox campaign, Custer's troops played a decisive role and Custer was on hand as General Lee surrendered. In fact, the table used to sign the article of surrender was given to Custer as a wedding gift and sits in the Custer Museum in Monroe.

Custer spent much of his boyhood living with his half-sister and bother in law in Monroe, Michigan. Custer married Elizabeth Bacon on February 9, 1864 whom he first met when he was 10 years old (although he was not socially introduced to her until 1862) Elizabeth's father, Judge Daniel Bacon disapproved of George as a match because he was the son of a blacksmith. It was not until well after George had been promoted to Major General that he gained the approval of Judge Bacon.

Monroe erected a statue of General Custer that sits in the center of town. The statue, selected by Elizabeth, was unveiled in 1910 by President William Howard Taft. The statue commemorates his successful actions during the Civil War and not his failures during the Indian campaign. The statue shows Custer wearing his Civil War fatigues, and since he did not die in the Civil War, the horse in the sculpture traditionally has all four legs on the ground. Folk lore states that one raised hoof indicates a rider wounded in battle, two raised hooves signifies death in battle, and all four hooves on the ground means the rider survived all battles unharmed.

"What do you think of Roosevelt's latest speech? It sounds ok but boy, will there ever be taxes. It'll be a little tough for everyone for the next year besides us but the sooner everything will be normal again."

With the end of World War 1, the United States adopted a policy of isolationism and non-interventionism. It even went so far as to not be a member in the League of Nations. Many Americans, remembering the horrors of World War 1, believed that our involvement was a mistake and were against any future intervention into European affairs. When Germany invaded Poland the United States was still committed to these goals. Despite the support of Roosevelt and a large percentage of the population, the strong isolationist movement in Congress ensured no substantial support would be provided our allies in Europe. By June of 1940, with the fall of France, Britain stool virtually alone against the German military. Winston Churchill called for Roosevelt and the United States to supply them with arms to continue their war effort.

In an address known as the "Four Freedoms Speech", Roosevelt proposed the four fundamental freedoms that people everywhere in the world should have. Roosevelt's hope was to provide a rationale for why the United States should abandon the isolationist policies that emerged from World War 1. The speech coincided with the introduction of the Lend Lease Bill, which promoted Roosevelt's plan to become the "arsenal of democracy" and support the allies with much needed supplies. Furthermore, the speech established what would become the ideological basis for American's involvement in World War 2.

The four freedoms as outlined by Roosevelt are as follows:

The freedom of speech and expression.

The freedom to worship God in his own way.

The freedom from want which means allowing every nation a healthy peacetime.

Finally, the freedom from fear which means a reduction of arms so that no nation can be in a position to commit aggression against another nation.

Roosevelt went on to explain that this world vision is the very opposite of the new order of tyranny proposed by the Axis forces. He added that a "good" society is able to face these schemes of world domination without fear. He then closed his speech by the commitment to those who

struggle to gain or keep their freedom.   "To that high
concept there can be no end save victory".

<u>JANUARY 8, 1942</u>

"I got to thinking about how tough people in civilian life will have it with taxes and rationing of tires and everything."

Rationing of items began and ended at different times
dependent upon their need for the military and their
availability.   Here is a list of some of the rationed items
and the years they were rationed:

Tires   January, 1942

Gasoline   May, 1942

Shoes   February, 1943

Sugar   May, 1942

Coffee   November, 1942

36

"I want to finish this letter by the time the Joe Louis fight comes on so I can listen to it."

Joe Louis fought a charity bout for Navy Relief Society against his former opponent Buddy Baer on January 9, 1942. The bout which lasted only one round as Louis knocked out Baer quickly, generated over 47,000 dollars. The next day, Louis volunteered to enlist as a private in the United States army. Newsreel cameras recorded his induction which included a staged scene where an army clerk asked Joe, "What is your occupation?" and Louis replied' "Fighting and let us at them Japs."

Louis was assigned to a segregated cavalry unit at Fort Riley in Kansas. He received this assignment because of his great affection for horses and at the suggestion of his friend and lawyer Truman Gibson. Gibson had become a civilian advisor to the War Department in charge of investigating claims of harassment against black soldiers. Accordingly, Louis used his personal connections to help the cause of various black soldiers with whom he came into contact. In one episode, Louis contacted Gibson in order to facilitate the Officer Candidate School application of a group of African Americans which had been inexplicably delayed several months. One of those applications belonged to Jackie Robinson and this intervention by Louis forged a lifelong friendship between the two men.

Realizing the potential for elevating the morale among the troops, the Army placed Louis in its Special Services Division rather than combat. Louis went on celebrity tours with other celebrities and traveled more than 21000 miles and gave nearly 100 boxing exhibitions in front of two million soldiers. In addition to his travels, Louis was the focus of a recruitment campaign encouraging African American men to enlist. When asked about his decision to enter the racially segregated United States Army, Louis explained "Lots of things are wrong with America, but Hitler ain't going to fix them." Louis had vast celebrity power outside of the African American segment of society. In a famous recruitment slogan showing Louis stating, "We'll win because we're on God's side" he was the first black man to be so widely embraced by white Americans.

Although he never saw combat, his military service would create many challenges for Louis. He often was the recipient of blatant racism during his travels, and on one occasion, a military policeman ordered Louis to move his seat to a bench in the rear of a bus. Louis replied "I ain't moving" and as the military policeman attempted to arrest him, Louis forcefully argued out of the situation. In another situation, Louis had to bribe a commanding officer to drop charges against Jackie Robinson for punching a captain who had called him a "nigger."

Louis was promoted to the rank of sergeant and awarded the Legion of Merit for "incalculable contribution to the general morale." Louis was honorably discharged on October 1, 1945.

JANUARY 15, 1942

"I bought $10.00 worth of defense stamps today and more on payday."

Defense stamps were a savings mechanism that allowed a person to purchase war bonds. War bond denominations started at $25.00 so an individual could purchase defense stamps and cash them in for war bonds when they had purchased sufficient amounts.

"Saturday night a guard over at our guard house put his gun at his heart and pulled the trigger."

The United States military did not track the suicide rate among soldiers during World War Two. However, this book notes two soldier suicides indicating there was a true issue that the military needed to confront, but avoided.

FEBRUARY 5, 1942

"All day yesterday and last night I had charge of a crew of guards who were guarding a long trestle and railroad bridge about 20 miles from here."

Thanks to its distance from the European, African, and Pacific theatres, the mainland United States never became a significant site of any sabotage during World War Two. But while North America was spared the destruction of total warfare, both the Germans and Japanese waged small scale campaigns of bombing, sabotage, and espionage on American soil which resulted in guard duties at bridges and other important installations.

FEBRUARY 10, 1942

"I'm listening to the radio right now and the British aren't doing worth a damn in the Far East. I guess it takes a Yank to do any good."

The battle of Singapore was fought when Japan invaded the stronghold of Singapore. Singapore was the major British military base in South East Asia and was called the "Gibraltar of the East". The fall of Singapore to the Japanese is considered one of the greatest defeats in the history of the British army. It also illustrated the way Japan was going to fight the war, a combination of speed and savagery. The surrender of Singapore demonstrated that the Japanese army was a force to be reckoned with and also ushered in years of appalling treatment for the British that were captured.

The Japanese onslaught took everyone by surprise. Speed was very important for the Japanese who never allowed the British forces time to regroup. The British had expected the Japanese to attack from the sea. Thus they placed all of their defenses along the shore. It was inconceivable that the Japanese would attempt an attack through the jungle and swamps of the Malay Peninsula.

However, this is the exact attack plan that the Japanese would execute.

As the Japanese attacked, their troops were ordered to take no prisoners because that would only slow down the Japanese advance. The orders provided to the Japanese were:

"When you encounter the enemy after landing, think of yourself as an avenger coming face to face at last with your father's murderer. Here is a man whose death will lighten your heart."

The Japanese advanced with 65,000 men lead my General Tomoyuki Yamashita. The British were led by General Arthur Percival and he had over 90,000 men, but they had never seen combat. On January 31, 1942, the British forces withdrew across the causeway that separated Singapore from Malaya. This was to be their final stand. It also proved to be a mistake as the British overestimated the strength of the Japanese and had spread out their forces too thinly in preparation for the attack.

On February 8, 1942 the final siege by the Japanese began with approximately 23,000 men. The Japanese advanced with speed and ferocity and the British never really were able to muster any resistance. The Japanese took 100,000 men prisoners, many of whom never fired a shot during the battle. The Japanese murdered any Chinese they encountered in the battle refusing to take them as prisoners. Of the British taken as prisoners, 9,000 would die constructing the Burma-Thailand railway for the Japanese.

The fall of Singapore was a humiliation for the British government. The Japanese were portrayed as useless soldiers and inferior to the might British Empire. Prior to the attack, Sir Winston Churchill stated, "There must be no thought of sparing the troops or population. Commanders and senior officers should die with their troops. The honor or the British Empire and British army is at stake." After the fall of Singapore, Churchill called it the "worst disaster and largest capitulation in British history.

FEBRUARY 17, 1942

"I saw in the paper where my old pal Red DeSloover is getting married. Another war scare."

At first the system did not draft married men, which led to a significant and inevitable "marriage boom". Fathers were not drafted until late in 1943 and it was over the protest of Senators that insisted "slackers" be drafted before American homes were broken up.

FEBRUARY 19, 1942

"They ought to give us a few days pretty soon, at least I hope so. If it were up to me, I'd be home. I don't mean that I'd get out if I could because I wouldn't want to get out before this is over and leave the rest of the guys do the battling."

FEBRUARY 22, 1942

"Today Carl and I had a chicken dinner at the Service club. They soaked us 85 cents but its good to eat out once in a while.

A similar dinner today costs upwards of eight dollars.

FEBRUARY 26, 1942

"I listened to the President but he didn't say much. Just tried to bolster morale up a little."

That speech is referred to Executive Order 9076 which was designed to do just as Marvin stated. It recognized military and non-military personnel for actions above and beyond the normal course of their duty for the war effort.

MARCH 4, 1942

"If I didn't tell you before, they're trying to make officers out of us non coms. We HAVE to make an application but the entrance tests are pretty hard so there's very small chance of any of us making it."

The United States Army's Officer Candidate School was located at Fort Benning, Georgia. The OCS is a rigorous twelve week course designed to train, assess, evaluate, and develop lieutenants for the army. General Omar Bradley is credited with establishing the format, discipline, and code of conduct for the OCS. Between July, 1941 and May, 1947, over 100,000 candidates were enrolled in the OCS, with approximately 27 percent completing the course and earning their commissions.

"I never knew what I got on my Army classification until last night. You had to have 110 to try to be an officer and 150 is a perfect score. Imagine my surprise when they told me my score was 143."

Marvin scored a 143 on the Armed Forces Vocational Aptitude Battery (ASVAB). The ASVAB is a mandatory test for all recruits. It has two primary purposes, the first being to determine if you have the mental aptitude necessary to enlist. The second to help determine what role you are best suited for in the military.

The test consists of 150 questions in the areas of vocabulary, arithmetic, and block counting. More than nine million men took the exam during World War Two and it indicated that only 63 percent could read or write above a third grade level.

MARCH 8, 1942

"I've got Gene Autry on and he's singing "I Paid My Income Tax Today." It reminded me of you forking over 14 bucks."

"It's a good thing you've got a few radios as I see that they'll stop making them next month. Everything has to go for production of instruments of war.

The electronic circuitry and elements required to construct a radio are identical to those used in the cockpit of airplanes.

MARCH 18, 1942

"There really is a lot of bustle when the air raid signal sounds. Fire engines running around with their sirens screaming, trucks and large guns scattering down the roads and under cover, men with rifles and machine guns taking up positions."

The United States Office of Civilian Defense, established in May of 1942 as the war continued to spread, was responsible for coordinating the preparations for war

48

related emergencies. It also made sure that everything was organized at the state and local levels. The civilian defense against air attacks began with pilots who flew along coastlines and plane spotters in towers watching for approaching enemy planes. There were blackout drills that forced people to practice their response to air raid signals and wardens who drove up and down streets to make sure no light escaped from any homes.

The blackout drills were planned in advanced and advertised. Street lights were turned off at a prescribed time and anyone outside was expected to take cover. Those in their homes were instructed to pull down all their blinds and keep any light inside to a minimum. People in cars had to pull over immediately and seek shelter in the nearest building.

The federal government sponsored advertisements to promote participation in the drills. There was even a song by Tony Pastor entitled "Obey Your Air Raid Warden" with the following lyrics:

"Don't get in a huff; Our aim today is to call their bluff; Follow these rules and that is enough; Obey your air raid warden."

In addition, posters were utilized to explain procedures and what required supplies should be kept on hand. Those supplies included fifty feet of garden hose with spray nozzle, 100 pounds of sand divided into four containers, three gallons of water, shovel, hoe, ax, ladder, gloves, and dark glasses.

MARCH 20, 1942

"All I can hope is that I get out of the army Ok and in short order. We'll be getting started against those slant eyed Japs before long and then it won't last long."

MARCH 24, 1942

"I've heard they won't tell us until the day before we leave as they fear sabotage of the trains. That is what happened in the wreck near Springfield a few weeks ago."

While it was never proven that sabotage was the cause of the train accident in Missouri, the newspaper account left some unanswered questions as to its cause. The accident was caused when two trains collided head on killing six and injuring over 45. Two of the dead were soldiers and two others were members of the Will Rogers team. Railway officials claimed a mix up in signals caused the crash, however, the true cause of the accident was never proven.

While it is uncertain if the accident truly was an act of sabotage, there were other proven attacks on United States soil by members of the Axis forces. On February 23, 1942, the Japanese submarine I-17 snuck into the channel of a large oil well and storage facility outside of Santa Barbara. It managed to fire sixteen shells before submerging and returning to the ocean. The damage was minimal but the implications were severe. This was the first shelling of the United States mainland and it caused panic among Americans regarding a possible invasion. The next day, reports of enemy aircraft led to the "Battle of Los Angeles" in which military artillery was fired due to the mistaken belief that the Japanese were invading.

The only attack on a mainland American military base in history occurred on June 21, 1942 when a Japanese I-25 submarine fired upon Fort Stevens. The submarine had trailed fishing vessels to bypass minefields and surfaced firing 17 shells at the fort. The Japanese aim was so poor, the commander of Fort Stevens ordered his men not to return fire as their flashes would reveal their position.

The same submarine would make history again, this time with the first ever bombing of the American mainland by an enemy aircraft. In what became known as the Lookout Air Raids, the I-25 launched a Yokosuka floatplane, piloted by Nobuo Fujita. The floatplane dropped a pair of incendiary bombs in the hope of starting a major forest fire near Brookings, Oregon and draw military resources away from the war effort. Thanks to light winds and quick response, the bombing mission failed.

After the war, Fujita, was invited to Brookings in 1962 and only made the trip when the Japanese government was assured he wouldn't be tried as a war criminal. Fujita brought with him a samurai sword that he intended to use on himself if given a hostile reception. Instead, the town treated him with respect and the sword sits in the town library. Fujita made several more goodwill visits to Brookings planting a tree at the bomb site as a gesture of peace. Fujita later acted as host to three Brookings students who visited Japan on his request and became an honorary citizen of the United States days before he died in 1997.

The largest invasion of American soil by the enemy came when eight Nazi saboteurs were sent to the United States on a doomed mission known as Operation Pastorius. The men were to sabotage the war effort and demoralize the citizens of the United States through acts of terrorism. The men were divided into two man teams with $84,000 in cash and enough explosives to wage a long campaign of sabotage. They had orders to attack transport hubs, power plants and industrial facilities. However, before a single act of sabotage could be committed, one of the saboteurs turned himself into the FBI. Saboteur George Dasch was heavily interrogated and after two weeks all of the remaining saboteurs were apprehended.

One of the more unusual military actions was the use of balloon bombs, or Fugos. The Japanese constructed and launched over 9,000 high altitude balloons, each loaded with nearly fifty pounds of explosives. After being launched, the balloons would rise to an altitude of 30,000 feet and ride the jet stream across the Pacific Ocean. Their bombs were triggered to drop after the three day journey was complete. Nearly 350 bombs made it across the Pacific Ocean with several being shot down by the military. The bombs were spotted in over fifteen states as far east as Michigan. The only casualty came from an incident in Oregon where six people were killed in an explosion from one of the downed balloons. Their deaths are the only combat casualties to occur on United States soil during World War Two.

"Guess who is going to be at the theater here in person for one week starting March 30. It's my old heartbeat, Ann Sheridan. I'm going to be in the front row every night."

Marvin probably wasn't alone in his feelings for Ann Sheridan and he surely had competition for those front row seats. Ann Sheridan won the "Search for Beauty" contest which carried with it a Paramount Studio screen test. She signed a contract under her real name of Clara Lou Sheridan, but, Paramount did little to develop her talent so she left and signed with Warner Brothers Studio as Ann Sheridan.

Warner Brothers billed her as the "Oomph Girl", a name which she despised. She was allowed to mature into a leading star and despite being in a number of forgettable movies, the public liked her and her career flourished.

MARCH 29, 1942

"I'm really going to be holy next week. A novena on Tuesday, confession Wednesday, mass on Thursday, and Tre Ore on Friday."

Tre Ore, or "The Three Hours of Agony" is a service held in Catholic churches on Good Friday from noon until 3 P.M. to commemorate the passion of Christ. It may include the seven sayings of Jesus on the Cross or the Stations of the Cross.

MAY 2, 1942

"They took 15 men from each battery and made a complete regiment out of them. We've a pretty good idea where they're going as they have their forwarding addresses already. That is if they get there safe but it is overseas. So you can see the war is touching pretty close to home."

MAY 24, 1942

"I see where the army and navy still need a lot of doctors so if you went to work for another one he might have to go also so where would you be?"

The United States created a system for the "Doctor Draft" aimed at including health professionals into military service. Unless otherwise exempted, these men could be called for up to 21 months of active duty and five years of reserve duty.

Bertha's employer, Dr. Vincent Barker was sworn in as a Lieutenant commander of the Navy Medical Corps and reported to the Great Lakes Naval Training Station where he was chief of surgery for more than a year. He was transferred to the Naval Hospital in Norman, Oklahoma where he was also chief of surgery. In 1945 he was sent overseas where he built a five hundred bed hospital on the island of Saipan in the Pacific.

JUNE 3, 1942

"That was pretty good about the British and Americans bombing Germany the other night. If they can do that a few times, there won't be much of Germany left."

The first 1,000 bomber raid by the United States was on May 30 and Cologne, one of Germany's largest cities, was the target. Codenamed Operation Millennium, it was hoped that the devastation from such a raid would knock Germany out of the war or severely damage the German morale. Hamburg was the original target, but bad weather forced a change in the plan.

This was the first time that a "bomber stream" was used, a tactic that was hoped to overwhelm the German defenses. By flying in a tightly packed stream, the German flak gunners could not discern the available targets.

During the raid, 868 aircraft dropped 1,455 tons of bombs starting over 2,500 fires. Nearly 13 thousand buildings were damaged to some extent and nearly 500 people were killed. Only 22 aircraft were lost in the mission allowing the military to call it a complete success.

JUNE 28, 1942

"If you keep hanging around the country club playing golf, you should be able to grab off some nice well to do young man, even if he is a 4-F"

Thirty percent of registrants in American were rejected for physical defects. The 4-F classification was given primarily for muscular and bone malformations, hearing or circulatory ailments, mental deficiency or disease, hernias, or syphilis. If you were 4-F you were considered "tainted goods". Some of the women commented, "Nobody wanted to date these boys who didn't pass their physicals and we called them 4-Fers." Another woman stated, "When I started college it was like a girl's school with 95 women and only 5 male students. By the time I graduated, several of the girls were dating high school seniors because the boys on campus were 4-F. They needed a good reason for not being in the service to be respected by the girls."

JULY 2, 1942

"Red and I plan to hitch hike to St. Louis Saturday. No kidding, but we make faster time by thumbing than by bus or train. Also manage to chisel a few drinks."

JULY 12, 1942

"I couldn't find a portable radio that was any good. They were all large ones that you could only get two or three stations. So I decided that as long as we had one radio in the family, we were all set."

"Now listen honey, the only reason I put that "if" in "if we get married" is that I may never come back if I go and that would be the only reason."

JULY 19, 1942

"I think they could end this war sooner if they would send me over."

Basic training lasted only a few months for most soldiers, however, the total training program could last up to two years.

AUGUST 8, 1942

"We had an 18 mile hike with full pack, rifle, and gas mask. It was pouring so we had to lug raincoats and heavy boots. They practically ran us for the first 5 miles before we had a rest and everyone was ready to quit then. From then on the men kept dropping off like flies but the sun came out and it really was hot. I've never seen guys suffer so before as every guy was in agony and dirty and wet with sweat. They'd just fall flat on their face and lay unable to move a muscle. I saw one that we passed and blood was coming out of his nose, eyes, and ears. Another just laid there twitching spasmodically. Norm Nadeau was walking in front of me and all of a sudden down he went in a heap. It was reported that 260 men reported to the medics after we got back. I wouldn't *give up even though I had cramps n both my legs the last mile."*

AUGUST 19, 1942

"I just heard a news flash over the radio that American forces had landed on the Solomon Islands which are held by Japan. They have a large naval base there and I hear that all we lost was one cruiser. It's about time that we started something to try and get this over with."

On August 7, 1942, Allied forces landed on the islands of Guadalcanal and Tulagi in the southern Solomon Islands with the objective of denying their use by the Japanese who utilized the islands to threaten supplies and communication between the United States, Australia, and New Zealand. The Allies overwhelmed the outnumbered Japanese defenders who had occupied the islands since May of 1942.

The Guadalcanal campaign was a significant strategic victory over the Japanese. The Japanese had been successful in their conquests in the Pacific and this marked the transition of the Allies from defensiveness to aggressiveness in the Pacific which resulted in the eventual surrender of Japan.

"I was wondering if you are doing anything for the war like volunteering for first aid or neighborhood fire warden."

If the United States was going to come under attack again, the military wasn't any help in calming the rising panic. Lt. General John DeWitt declared, "This is war. Death and destruction may come from the skies at any moment." When asked by a reporter if the United States was open to enemy attack, President Roosevelt replied. "Enemy ships could swoop in and shell New York; enemy planes could drop bombs on war plants in Detroit; enemy troops could attack Alaska." When one reporter asked whether the Army or Navy and Air Force were strong enough to deal with situations like that, Roosevelt replied, "Certainly not." It was even suggested that the White House be painted black to make it harder for enemy planes to spot.

Every school practiced air raid drills after viewing news reels of the Japanese bombings of China and the German bombings in Europe. There is no doubt that American cities would have been targeted by Germany if the war had lasted longer. In addition to practice at schools, families would conduct drill at home during the evening. The government had advised each family to have an emergency supply kit containing blankets, candles, matches, canned food, and water. California was extremely cautious due to the attack on Pearl Harbor and instituted strict black out regulations.

Women did everything from building airplanes to planting victory gardens during World War Two. Some women worked in factories operating large machinery while others were trained to fly the completed aircraft to their final destinations. Other women took on more traditional female jobs sewing aircraft upholstery or painting radium on dials for night vision. And still others volunteered selling bonds, donating blood, salvaging goods, or sending care packages overseas.

AUGUST 20, 1942

"I see the allies are opening up at last as according to the radio they are blasting France and preparing for a second front soon. I wish I could be with the marines as they are really seeing action and plenty."

American flying fortresses raided areas in occupied France and it was the first all American bomber raid over enemy territory carried out from a base in Britain. The bombers were escorted by British fighters and additional raids over enemy territory would be combined with the Royal Air Force.

The Dieppe Raid, also known as the Battle of Dieppe, was code named Operation Jubilee. It was the second attack on the port of Dieppe and began the morning of August 19. The objective of the raid was to prove it was possible seize and hold a major port to and to gain intelligence from prisoners and captured material. The raid did not meet any of these objectives and only provided a morale boost to the public. Over 3000 of the troops who stormed Dieppe were either killed, wounded, or captured. The Royal Air Force lost 96 planes and the Royal Navy lost 33 landing craft.

The Dieppe Raid provided some relief from the Soviet government who strongly wanted a second front to be created. Joseph Stalin himself demanded that the allies create a second front in France to divert German resources away from the Eastern Front and remove some of the pressure from the Soviet Army.

An interesting side note is that an additional secret mission was conducted on Dieppe by the British. The name of their team was "No. 30 Commandos" and they were created to operate with forward troops for the sole purpose of seizing documents and carry out interrogations. Their mission at Dieppe was to steal one of the new German 4 rotor Enigma code machines plus code books and rotor setting sheets. One of the key figures involved in the creation of this unit was Ian Flemming, author of the James Bond novels. Unfortunately, no coding machine was recovered in this raid.

"I got a small carton containing 4 packages of cigarettes from the I.O.O.F., K of C and those others who have started that campaign, "Cigs for Yanks". Then I got another carton this afternoon."

Smoking in the United States military really began with World War One when tobacco companies began to target military personnel through the distribution of cigarettes to servicemen and the eventual inclusion of cigarettes into ration kits. During World War Two, cigarettes were a mainstay in a soldier's life. They appeared in their rations and were either smoked for a bit of relaxation or sold on the black market. Tobacco companies enjoyed the soldiers smoking through World War Two as it meant nicotine addiction and the guaranteed purchase of cigarettes when the war ended.

AUGUST 29, 1942

"What I wouldn't give to have this war over with so I could be free again and do whatever I wanted to. Personally I don't think that it will last too much longer and I hope everything goes as I hope it will."

SEPTEMBER 30, 1942

"Bet on the Yankees in the World Series as I've seen the Cardinals play."

The World Series featured the defending champion New York Yankees against the St Louis Cardinals. The Cardinals won the series in five games for their first championship since 1934 and fourth overall.

OCTOBER 28, 1942

"*The conductor was telling us about a soldier who the night before on the same train got drunk while on the way back to camp. He was brooding about his troubles and finally jumped off the train which was going 80 miles per hour.*"

NOVEMBER 2, 1942

"*This camp is under black out conditions all night as being so close to the ocean. All of the lights have shades around them so that they deflect the light straight down and they have huge search lights shooting beams all over the sky every now and then.*"

While army and navy installations along the coast were under blackout restrictions, coastal communities were not. Many coastal towns resisted the imposition of a blackout fearing a loss of tourism. The result was a disastrous loss of shipping as the lit coastline served to silhouette any ships in the area. The German submarine crews called it "American shooting season". During this "American shooting season", German submarines sank a total of 609 ships and loss only 22 U-boats.

NOVEMBER 9, 1942

"That was pretty good news about the U.S. forces landing in Africa. Sort of a surprise but there will be plenty of those before very long. I hope it continues."

The raid in North Africa was done to appease the Soviets and Joseph Stalin who pleaded for a second military front. The Americans wanted a landing in occupied Europe (code named Operation Sledgehammer) but the British thought such a mission would end in disaster. The compromise mission was a raid on North Africa (code named Operation Torch) to clear the Axis powers from North Africa, give the allies control of the Mediterranean Sea, and prepare the Allies for an invasion of southern Europe in the future.

General Eisenhower was given command of Operation Torch and his plan was to invade Sicily from Northern Africa. Then he was planned on marching into Italy and control the entire Mediterranean Sea. The Allies invaded Morocco and Algeria which were under nominal rule of

Vichy France. As the Vichy government in France was seen as collaborators with the Nazi's, they were both seen as legitimate targets.

The key to the success of Operation Torch was a successful amphibious landing. Three landing sites were chosen, Oran, Algiers, and Casablanca. General George Patton was chosen to command the landing at Casablanca. The landings started before daybreak without air or naval bombardment as the Allies did not expect any resistance from the French. The capture of Casablanca was seen as a key target for the invasion and Patton took the city two days after his landing.

The landings at all three beaches were extremely successful. The landing at Oran damaged the landing craft due to the shallow water and the timing of the tide. This proved to be very beneficial when plans were made for the invasion of France known as D Day. The planners made sure the landing craft would not encounter the possibility of becoming damaged or grounded in what was expected to be a fierce fight.

"I went to the early show. The picture was "Road to Morocco" with Bing Crosby."

They were called the "road pictures", a series of comedies starring Bing Crosby and Bob Hope made over the course of twenty years by Paramount Pictures. They contained a mix of comedy gags, musical numbers, exotic locations, and ad lib banter from two on screen and off screen friends.

The original screenplay for the first film, "The Road to Singapore" was originally written for George Burns and Gracie Allen. However, they turned it down and the idea of pairing Bing Crosby with Bob Hope created one of the most famous movie franchises. The films always included references to other actors, jabs at Paramount, and Bob Hope's comments directly to the audience. His most famous is when he advises the audience during the "Road to Bali', "Crosby's gonna sing now folks, now's the time to go out and get the popcorn."

The movie plots were almost always the same. Both characters would promise not to allow women to interfere with their plans, and then both would see a woman and forget the pledge. Crosby always wound up with the girl.

Hope's character always had a silly nickname and he would attempt to have dialogue with the audience while continuously over acting. He would always blame his over acting on his zealous attempt to win the Oscar.

An eighth "Road" picture was planned in 1977, "The Road to the Fountain of Youth", but was never made as Bing Crosby died that year.

JANUARY 3, 1943

"I tried to call home but after waiting five hours I got very disgusted and got ready for inspection."

FEBRUARY 2, 1942

"I slept until 11:00 this morning and the maid didn't get a chance to clean up my room. Yeah, can you imagine that we pay 10 cents a day and have a colored maid that makes our beds and cleans our room."

FEBRUARY 7, 1942

"I don't usually smoke cigarettes but they send them so I'm considerate and use them up."

The Department of Defense calculated that smoking in the military was 150% higher than that of civilians. Because of this statistic, it discontinued the inclusion of cigarettes in K rations. There have been some calculations that have indicated that the possible number of cancer deaths due to the creation of a smoking habit during World War Two is approximately 780,000 while the number of war related deaths totaled slightly more than 292,000.

FEBRUARY 15, 1943

"We have a new arrival in the outfit that I was in. He's the movie star Tom Brown. Maybe you remember Jeffrey Lynn of the movies. Well, he flunked out of OCS."

As a child model from two years old, Tom Brown posed as Buster Brown, the Arrow Collar Boy, and the Buick Boy. He is best known for his roles in "The Adventures of Smilin Jack" and "Anne of Green Gables".

Brown was carried on stage by his mother at the age of six months. He was educated at the New York Professional Children's School prior to enlisting in the army. He served as a paratrooper and later also served in the Korean War where he became a lieutenant colonel.

Jeffrey Lynn was a school before he began his acting career. He had his big break in 1938 when he appeared with the Lane Sisters in the movie "Four Daughters." The movie was such a great hit that it spawned three sequels. After the success of these movies, he screen tested for the role of Ashley Wilkes in the classic "Gone With the Wind." He was considered the front runner for the role because of his resemblance to the character as portrayed in the novel.

In fact, Lynn was used extensively in the "Search for Scarlett" screen tests, playing Ashley for the many actresses who tried out for the role of Scarlett. Unfortunately, the role of Ashley was eventually given to the more experienced and popular actor, Leslie Howard.

FEBRUARY, 22, 1943

"I saw Madam Chiang Kai Shek in the newsreel and just now some guy was talking about her on the radio. She's really a great woman and really can talk."

It was early in 1943 and the Republic of China was struggling to resist the invading Japanese army. Soong Mei-ling, the wife of Gereralissimo Chaing Kai-Shek was in the United States for medical reasons. Madame Chaing Kai Shek seized the opportunity and began urging the United States to side with her country. During a five month period, Madame Chain Kai Shek traveled the United States from New York to San Francisco giving speeches regarding her country's plight. It was her address to Congress that truly made her remarkable in the eyes of the United States public. She was described by radio commentators as "the personification of China" as she spoke to the country looking slim and graceful. She wooed the listeners with a blend of compliments, barbs, and assertions as she stated "We in China are convinced that it is the better half of wisdom not to accept failure ignominiously, but to risk it gloriously." One congressman later stated, I never saw anything like it. Madame Chaing had me on the verge of bursting into tears."

Madame Chaing was educated at Wellesley College where she graduated in 1917. She was more than the wife of a Chinese leader. She had become the symbol of Chinese resistance. She was brave, articulate, and elegant as she lectured the world. Newspapers in the United States called her the most powerful woman in the world. Winston Churchill might have said it best when he called her "remarkable and charming" and that she mixed "sex with politics". Being remarkable, charming, and sexy were obviously very formidable as Time magazine put her on its cover three times.

MARCH 22, 1943

"We are allowed 200 miles a day by car and it was about 750 miles to Lexington so that gave us four days. Plus we are allowed 8 cents per mile."

This was the number of miles the government anticipated would be traveled daily in the course of business. It is incredible to realize that the average distance traveled by car in a day easily exceeds 700 miles!

APRIL 5, 1943

"Another thing, I am going on a trip for a week or maybe two. They send out valuable signal equipment every two or three days. One officer and a few men go along in a caboose and guard the cars until the goods are delivered. There are five shipments going out any time now and we four here are each slated to go with one. We have to keep in touch with the post no matter where we go as we may leave at any minute. We don't know the where as we are given sealed orders and don't open them until after we are on the way."

APRIL 11, 1943

"What a time but I'm on my way back. I couldn't let you know as we were under secret orders. I had 4 guards besides myself to take three cars of equipment to the port of embarkation at Norfolk, VA. We rode in the caboose all the way. I had my hands full as I had to get provisions, ammunition, blankets, papers, and keep a running log of the whole journey. I also had to telegraph back the time of my arrival and send back by registered mail the log of the trip in triplicate."

The mission involved the delivery of coding equipment for shipment overseas to various American bases and installations in the European theatre of operation. The need for secrecy and utmost security was crucial as it would have been disastrous if the coding devices had been obtained by the axis forces.

APRIL 15, 1943

"I got a carton of Camels from the gang at Woodall. Guess I'll have to smoke them up."

APRIL 22, 1943

"Do you know that I've bought three bonds this month. The soldiers are not only fighting the war, but financing it too."

MAY 3, 1943

"The President really got his temper up regarding the miners and John L. Lewis and it's about time he got tough with them."

President Roosevelt addressed the nation giving his viewpoint on the miner strikes happening throughout the nation. In it he addressed the miners specifically stating: "I am speaking tonight to the American people, and in particular to those of our citizens who are coal miners. Tonight this country faces a serious crisis. We are engaged in a war on the successful outcome of which will depend the whole future of our country. This war has reached a new critical phase. After years of preparation, we have moved into active and continuing battle with our enemies. We are pouring into the worldwide conflict everything that we have, our young men, and the vast resources of our nation."

President Roosevelt wasn't done letting the citizens of the United States know exactly how he felt about the striking miners when he concluded his speech by saying:

"I want to make it clear that every American coal miner who has stopped mining coal, no matter how sincere his motives, no matter how legitimate he may believe his grievances to be, every idle miner directly and individually is obstructing our war effort. We have not yet won this war. We will win this war only as we produce and deliver our total American effort on the high seas and on the battlefronts. And that requires unrelenting, uninterrupted effort here on the home front. A stopping of the coal supply, even for a short time, would involve a gamble with the lives of American soldiers and sailors and the future security of our whole people. It would involve an unwarranted, unnecessary, and terribly dangerous gamble with our chances for victory. Therefore, I say to all miners, and to all Americans everywhere, at home and abroad, the production of coal will not be stopped."

There were many signs that the mining community was growing tired of their plight. The coal miners worked in primarily small towns and were suffering a mix of unemployment and poor wages. When the Pennsylvania miners walked off their jobs in January of 1943, it was clear that their revolt had begun.

On March 10, the United Mine Workers had presented the mine owners demands that included a 35 hour, five day work week and a $2.00 per hour raise. The union had cited a horrific accident rate that included 64,000 men killed and injured since 1941, 75,000 in 1942, and almost 100,000 in 1943 due to intensified production for the war. The owners refused to the terms and President Roosevelt pressed the Union to reduce its demands.

President Roosevelt himself intervened in the negotiations asking the owners to extend the contract and make any wage increases retroactive. He also stated that the dispute must be settled "under the no strike agreement" and final determination of the contract by the National War Labor Board.

On April 22, the War Labor Board announced it was assuming jurisdiction over the issue. The United Mine Workers refused to appear before a board that "was packed against labor." The War Labor Board announced two days later that it was settling the matter within the framework of the Little Steel Formula which ruled out any wage increases for the miners.

As more miners walked off their jobs, President Roosevelt was forced to step forward and take responsibility for leading the opposition against the miners. President Roosevelt telegraphed Lewis on April 29 and advised that he would "use all the powers vested in me as President and Commander in Chief of the Army and Navy" if the strikes were not ended by May 1. The mine workers response was to have an additional 10,000 miners in Ohio walk off their jobs. By the next day, every coal mine in the country was closed.

The press was unified in its hatred for Lewis and the miners. Volumes of slanders and threats were issued and Lewis was linked to Hitler in the newspapers, radio, and newsreels. On May 1, President Roosevelt himself ordered the government seizure of all mines that were closed due to strikes. The American flag was to be flown over the mines and the government directed the mines be run as agents for the government. The government ordered the striking miners back to work, however, none returned to the mines.

"What do you think of these coal strikes? They really burn me up. I'd like to take a bunch of men with machine guns and burn their pants off. We're going to make a suggestion to Frank that he draft every miner and then put them back to work in the mines with a few tough sergeants over them."

As the government attempted to keep the mines operating the miners remained steadfast in their strike. The strikers were unfazed at the thought of the army taking over the mines by saying, "you can't dig coal with bayonets."

President Roosevelt was out of options. He could not arrest over 500,000 miners nor could he force them to return to the mines at bayonet point. And even if he forced them back into the mines, he couldn't make them mine an ounce of coal. He considered arresting John L. Lewis, but the miners swore they would strike "until hell froze over" if Lewis were victimized in any fashion.

In the end, finally on November 20, the miners settled the strike that threatened the success of the war and divided the public. The miners received their demand of a two dollar per day raise in their base pay plus received forty dollars of retroactive travel time.

JUNE 14, 1942

"Just a quick line to let you know I'm taking a shipment of secret equipment to California. I'm due to leave at 9:30 P.M. tonight. Will probably be back around June 30."

The trip was a shipment of radio equipment to the west coast. The radios were specially designed to allow for longer range and clearer reception and were to be utilized as the American forces began to create a foothold in the Asia Theatre of Operation.

JULY 7, 1943

"There are thousands who are having worse burden to carry because of this war. At least our families and us are alive yet."

The total number of casualties from the war through June of 1943 was already in excess of 60,000.

AUGUST 12, 1943

"I shouldn't tell you this but I guess it won't hurt. We got our orders today and we are suppose to be ready so we are getting all our equipment. We are in the dark as to where we are going but it is an eastern port."

Ok, coded message, *"I am being shipped overseas."*

AUGUST 23, 1943

"I found some flashlight batteries and mailed them to Clayt today."

Many retailers welcomed rationing because they were already experiencing shortages of many items due to the rumors and panics, such as flashlight batteries after the attack on Pearl Harbor.

SEPTEMBER 16, 1943

"I really don't know what to write about as there are so many things we can't say anything about. It's a good thing we had that week end in Cinci as we may not see each other for a while."

NOVEMBER 3, 1943

"We got paid the other day and they paid us in francs. The higher the amount of money the larger the size the bill. Their 1000 frank note is the size of this paper."

5 inches by 7 inches!

NOVEMBER 4, 1943

"We haven't found out yet just what we are allowed to tell but all we could disclose would be which continent we are in. For that matter I don't think we are due to stay in this one."

"I know I'm never going to take another ocean voyage as long as I live (only the one back to the U.S.). It was nice to see land after so many days of seeing nothing but water. I know how Columbus must have felt."

NOVEMBER 8, 1943

"There isn't much that we can tell about without disclosing our exact location. I sent you a cable but all cables from North Africa are sent from one place so that doesn't mean anything."

NOVEMBER 13, 1943

"We got our weekly ration today. Mine consisted of 2 candy bars, 6 cigars, 2 packs of gum, 1 bar of soap, and a pack of razor blades. What I wouldn't do for a coca cola or any soft drink."

"It's quite a problem getting into a restaurant. You go in and ask the proprietor in the afternoon and he gives you a pass. You come back around 8 P.M. and they have a guard at the door and you have to show your pass to get in. Most of them are officers or French civilians."

NOVEMBER 20, 1943

"Every 5 feet any GI has 2 or 3 little Arab brats grabbing at his pants crying "shoe shine, goot American polish." That's the extent of their knowledge of English. We took a hike the other day and had about 20 kids following along side crying for bon bons and chewing gum."

90

DECEMBER 8, 1943

"We are on the move again but we don't know where but if we did I couldn't say anything anyhow."

"We've had plenty of excitement and I'm not kidding anyone when I say that I was praying to myself like I never did before. We can't tell anything about it now but we may be able to later. Remember two dates November 26 and November 29."

His Majesty's Troopship Rohna was carrying U.S. troops when it was sunk in an attack by the German Luftwaffe on November 26, 1943. The ship was part of a convoy that was attacked by approximately 30 bombers. The Rohna was the only ship in the convoy to sustain any damage.

However, the damage was dreadful. A total of eleven hundred men were lost of which over a thousand were Americans. The attack constituted the largest loss of U.S. troops at sea in a single incident. An additional 35 men died later from wounds incurred during the attack. The heavy loss was due in part to a flotilla of empty barge craft that failed to stop and pick up survivors, for which the commanding officer was relieved of his command.

In February of 1944, the U.S. government had acknowledged that over 1000 soldiers had been lost in the sinking of an unnamed troopship in European waters and hinted that it was the victim of a submarine attack. The reason for the suggestion that the attack was the work of a submarine, was because this was the first successful use of a remote controlled rocket boosted bomb by the Germans.

The Germans had begun building and testing guided missiles since 1940. The concept was to allow the plane to drop the bomb while out of enemy gun fire range and have the pilot control the missile to its intended target. Colored flares or flashing lights were attached to the bomb to make it visible to the pilot. Only after recovering the controlling device from a downed Nazi plane were the Allies able to create a means of neutralizing the missile. Not only was this the greatest loss of troops at sea by the United States (more than the USS Arizona at Pearl Harbor), it introduced the missile age to the war.

The event was so devastating that the government placed a veil of secrecy on it. The details of the loss were revealed slowly over time and were only released in full in 1967 after the introduction of the Freedom of Information

Act. On October 22, 2000, House Concurrent Resolution 408 recognized those that perished in the attack.

DECEMBER 19, 1943

"You don't know how lucky anyone is to live in the U.S. if you could only see the rest of this world. Filth, disease, poverty and such are everywhere. I'm actually going to kneel and kiss the good earth when I land back on the good shore."

JANUARY 10, 1944

"The war department has turned back 20,000 soldiers who have passed their preliminary cadet (aviation) exams because they don't need any more pilots. We had some men over here who were supposed to go back to the states for training but they were recalled after they were just ready to board the ship back."

JANUARY 14, 1944

"I have my own bearer who waits on me hand and foot. He wakes us in the morning, makes our bed, shines our shoes, lays out our under clothes, brushes off our clothes, takes care of our mending, tailoring, and laundry, brings us tea and papers, gets us tickets to shows, opens our beer, serves drinks, and a few other things."

JANUARY 15, 1944

"Joe E. Brown put on a show here the other day. He's a darn good sport and helped cheer the boys up a lot."

Joe E. Brown was an American actor and comedian remembered for his amiable persona, comic timing, and enormous smile.   He was one of the most popular comedians in the 1930's and 1940's.

Joe E. Brown began making movies in 1928 and quickly shot to stardom. He starred in a number of lavish musical comedies for Warner Brothers becoming such a star that his name began to appear alone above the movie title. From 1933 to 1936 he became one of the top earners in the film industry and became an international celebrity as well.

In 1939, Brown testified before the House Immigration Committee in support of a bill that would allow 20,000 German Jewish refugee children into the United States, adopting two of them himself. He traveled thousands of miles at his own expense to entertain the American troops before Bob Hope toured or the USO was created. On his return to the United States he would bring back sacks of letters making sure they got delivered. He performed in any weather, in hospitals, and even performed an entire show for a single dying soldier. Everyone who wanted an autograph received one.

Joe E. Brown was too old to enlist in the service, but both of his sons were in the military. He lost his son, Captain Donald Brown, in 1942 from a military plane crash. Brown was one of only two civilians to be awarded the Bronze Star in World War Two.

JANUARY 17, 1944

"The day of days finally arrived. We got all of our mail yesterday and it dated all the way back to September. I received 113 letters plus 7 more today. It must have taken me 5 hours to read them all but now I have a fair idea of what's been going on."

It was a challenge to follow the military personnel as they moved from theatre to theatre.

JANUARY 20, 1944

"I am just sitting here in my underclothes with all the windows open. Perhaps some kind hearted mosquito will take a nip at me so I can get malaria and go back to the U.S. Personally I don't look to be back any earlier than after I have put in 2 to 2 1/2 years overseas. They've named this place correctly when they called it CBI. That stands for Confused Bastards of India."

CBI was actually an umbrella term for the China, Burma, India Theater used by the United States military during

World War Two for the China and Southeast Asian or India-Burma theaters.

JANUARY, 29, 1944

"I was looking in a store window the other day and a native Indian was standing behind me. I didn't notice him but all of a sudden he let out a blood curdling yell and fell in a heap on the sidewalk. He laid there on his back with his feet in the air and his entire body shaking and froth coming out of his mouth. I didn't know what was coming off for a minute as lots of times these Indians go temporarily insane and run amuck. He either had an epileptic fit or was the result of malaria."

FEBRUARY 9, 1944

"I've rented a bicycle to go around on now a days. It only costs me five cents a month and I get plenty of exercise."

FEBRUARY 21, 1944

"There are going to be a lot of post war problems to be settled and it will take a lot of common sense on everyone's part to arrive at an amiable solution. For instance, I'm overseas for 2 years. There's no doubt that I'll change some for the better I hope. I'm living one kind of life in the army while your life is altogether different. Now it will be up to the individuals to think about those issues and plan to meet them when they arrive."

The divorce rate in 1946 was more than double the rate in 1940. Experts suggested that the issues ranged from caring for an incapacitated veteran to women not wanting to give up their newly found freedom.

In addition to the problems of those who were committed to one another, there was the problem of the "war brides" or "allotment Annies". These women hustled departing soldiers into marriage just to collect the fifty dollars a month paid to wives of servicemen. Some "Annies" took on as many as six husbands and those with financial talents specialized in airmen in hopes of collecting the life insurance.

APRIL 12, 1944

"I see women outnumber men in the U.S. by 500,000. I think I will reconsider marrying you and do a little shopping when I return."

In 1941 the total number of military personnel was slightly over 1,800,000. By 1945 that number had grown to over 12,000,000.

APRIL 17, 1944

"If I manage to get home before the war is over and get enough time, we'll get married. But conditions at that time may not warrant a large reception as feasible. A reception just isn't without beer and all and it may not be possible to get."

"Paulette Goddard is probably back in the U.S. by now as she left a few days ago. She didn't put on her show here as she was taken ill but she's a great girl for at least coming. I was introduced to her by a friend of mine at the hotel where she was staying. "

Paulette Goddard was a child fashion model and later was a performer in several Broadway productions as a Ziegfeld Girl. She became a major star at Paramount Studios and was nominated for an Academy Award for her performance in "So Proudly We Hail."

Paulette was the daughter of Alta Mae Goddard and Joseph Russell Levy, the son of a prosperous Jewish cigar manufacturer. The marriage did not last very long and Paulette was forced to relocate often by her mother to avoid custody battles. Paulette began modeling early in her childhood working for Saks Fifth Avenue. It was while working in New York that she was introduced to Broadway producer Florence Ziegfled and she began her Broadway career as a dancer.

Soon after, Goddard was introduced to Edgar James, President of the Southern Lumber Company located in

Asheville, North Carolina. Though she was only 16, she married him anyway with the marriage lasting barely three years. Goddard then moved to Hollywood where she appeared in only one film. With her film career seemingly over before it could even get started, she got a big break.

Paulette began dating film comedian Charlie Chaplin and the relationship started receiving national attention from the press. Charlie cast her as his leading lady in his box office hit "Modern Times" and she received rave reviews. Chaplin wanted to cast her in his next movie, but he was moving to slow for the ambitious Goddard. Worried that the public would forget about her, she signed a contract with David O. Selznick. Her movie "The Women" launched the movie career she had longed for.

Selznick was so thrilled with Goddard's performance he considered her for the role of Scarlet O'Hara. The initial screen tests convinced him that Goddard would require extensive coaching to be effective in the role. However, it was the opinion of Russell Birdwell, the head of Selznick's publicity department that might have doomed the role for Goddard. Birdwell warned Selznick of the "tremendous amount of criticism that will befall us and the picture should Paulette be given this part...I have never known a woman, intent on a career dependent upon her popularity with the masses, to hold and live such an insane and absurd attitude towards the press and her fellow man as does Paulette Goddard...Briefly, I think she is dynamite that will explode in our very faces if she is given the part." It was suggested that Goddard lost the part because Selznick feared questions surrounding her marital status with Charlie Chaplin would cause a scandal. However, Janet Leigh flourished was living with Laurence Olivier as their respective spouses refused to grant them a divorce.

Goddard moved on to Paramount Pictures where she starred in a movie with Bob Hope and joined Charlie Chaplin in his move "The Great Dictator". She divorced Chaplin in 1942 receiving a very generous settlement. She starred with Fred Astaire in the musical "Second Chorus" where she met husband number three, Burgess Meredith.

MAY 1, 1944

"I understand they are really calling everyone up to be examined for the draft. I hope Clayt doesn't pass because of his asthma as the army doesn't need all the men they've got now."

<u>June 21, 1944</u>

"The news of the invasion was Ok but we have our own war to fight over here. Don't look for. Germany to fall before late 1944 or early 1945. Japan not before 1946. These new B-29's sure are honeys though and may help end it sooner."

The B-29 Superfortress was a four engine propeller driven heavy bomber designed by Boeing. It was one of the largest aircraft to see service in World War Two and the most advanced bomber of its time with features like a pressurized cabin, electronic fire control system, and remote controlled machine gun turrets. The name "Superfortress" was derived from its predecessor, the B-17 Flying Fortress. Though it was designed as a high altitude daytime bomber, it was used extensively as a low altitude bomber at night.

The manufacturing of the B-29 was complex as it involved four factories located in Kansas, Georgia, and two in Washington employing thousands of subcontractors. There were two prototypes built and the modifications often happened so quickly that the plane would be flown directly to the modification depot. The modification depots had so much difficulty dealing with the size of the aircraft, the lack of hangars, and the weather that only fifteen of the one hundred built were considered air worthy. This poor production prompted General Hap Arnold to lead a team of production personnel to resolve the situation. This resulted in 150 aircraft becoming ready to fly within six weeks.

The invasion that Marvin feels went "OK" is commonly referred to as "D-Day". The landings were conducted in two phases, an airborne assault consisting of 24,000 troops shortly after midnight of June 6 and the amphibious landing that began at 6:30. The element of surprise was achieved due to the inclement weather and a comprehensive deception plan put in force months before the invasion. Operation Bodyguard convinced the Germans that the landings would take place to the north. There were in fact two operations code named Glimmer and Taxable that had distracted the Germans from the true landing areas. The main reason for the success of this diversion was Operation Fortitude South which convinced Hitler that the main attack was to be across the Straights of Dover led by General George Patton. The fiction was maintained so well that after the landings had begun Hitler was still convinced of its validity and refused to reinforce troops at Normandy. The utilization of bombers flying precise patterns over the Straights and dropping aluminum strips created a picture on German radar of an advancing fleet.

The invasion was the largest amphibious invasion in history and included 160,000 soldiers that attacked the beaches and 197,000 navy personnel in over 5,000 ships. Everything hinged on the weather which allowed only ten suitable days for a landing each month due to the necessity of a full moon and the correct tide. The weather began deteriorating on June 4 and it appeared as though the invasion would have to be postponed. General Eisenhower's chief meteorologist predicted a small window during the morning of June 6 and the rest is history.

General Eisenhower transmitted a message to the troops, saying in part, "You are about to embark upon the great crusade, toward which we have striven these many months." He also had a statement to be used if the operation failed that obviously was never used.

JUNE 28, 1944

"Friday night we went up to Darrel Berrigan's apartment to celebrate Cox's going home. Berrigan is a United Press correspondent who walked out of Burma with Stillwell."

"One of our captains who was due to go home in a few weeks so he sent his wife a telegram, quote, "When I get off the boat there's going to be a lot of f@#$ing on. If you want to get in on it, you better be there.""

JULY 3, 1944

"I can't tell you exactly where we are but we can get a nice view of the Himalayas."

JULY 16, 1944

"Jim Slamin, a lieutenant that I work with has only received one letter from his girlfriend who he's engaged to since April 28th. It looks like another one of those sad events that have been so numerous over here."

106

While there is no accurate record or accounting for the number of "Dear John" instances that occurred during the war, there is an amusing story about the situation. Private Clifford Elliot created "Love Insurance, LTD" and sold monthly policies to soldiers for a mere twenty five cents. The first soldier to lose his girlfriend collected the pool which averaged approximately $15.00.

"I have been getting quite a few newspapers in the mail. Lynch and I were very disappointed in the delivery of the comics as we were right up to the point where they were going to nab "Flat Top" and then we get the edition where "The Brow" is introduced. We are on pins and needles waiting to see what happened to Flat Top."

Dick Tracy was a hard hitting intelligent police detective created by Chester Gould. The comic strip made its debut on October 4, 1931 in the Detroit Mirror. The comic often had violence and the cases usually ended in a shootout. Gould created many villains for Tracy to apprehend and the most popular was Flattop Jones, a freelance hit man. The wrist radio was introduced on January 13, 1946, nearly sixty years before it became a reality.

The Brow was a Nazi spy who was monitoring ship movements and radioing the information back to his superiors. His most prominent physical traits are the pronounced brow ridges on his forehead and his lack of ears.

Dick Tracy arrested the Brow's subordinate, Spy 26 but the most damning evidence was lost and discovered by two sisters, May and June Summer. The Brow captured the two sisters and forced them to cooperate by placing one of them inside his "spike machine", and insidious machine that drove spikes into the victim's legs. June managed to free her sister from the machine and the two led Dick Tracy to The Brow's hideout. The Brow had managed to escape by hiding in his own diabolical device incurring much pain in the process. He waited patiently for revenge and while Tracy was having the sisters transported do a safe house, The Brow shot and killed the taxi driver and forced the cab off a bridge into a river drowning both girls.

The Brow now focused on getting revenge by killing Tracy's girlfriend, Sergeant Tess Truheart. By tracking down gas rationing coupons that blew out of her purse, The Brow stole her license plates to use for his next and final crime. However, Tracy was already closing in and a gun fight ensued at a nearby farm. Tracy was wounded when he was speared by a lightning rod thrown at him by The Brow. The Brow incurred massive head injuries while being shot at when trying to drive away. The blood blinded him and he drove into a gravel pit where he was tended to by a ghastly looking woman named Gravel Gertie who possessed a velvet voice. Unable to see her horrid features from his injuries, The Brow allowed her to hide him from the police and treat his wounds with a mixture of soot and spider webs.

The Brow was now madly in love with his doctor and rescuer by listening to her voice, however, upon removing his bandages he was horrified at her features. He tried to escape but she stopped him and in the struggle, The Brow set her house on fire. Gertie ran from the house and into a pond where she was found by Tracy who spotted The Brow running from the house. Tracy caught him and began pummeling him for the injury he sustained earlier and the killing of the two sisters. While being questioned at police headquarters, The Brow managed to steal a gun from a passing officer. While trying to release the safety, Tracy threw an ink well at The Brow causing him to fall backward out of a window to his death by being impaled by a flagpole bearing the flag of the country he tried to harm.

JULY 24, 1944

"For my work of recent months I have been recommended for a promotion. An officer does have to be recommended first though before they can promote him. All I want Is one as they are very hard to get over here."

JULY 28, 1944

"The cricket season seems to be here as every night our room is swarming in with them. On it top of that we can't keep anything around that is edible of its full of ants."

"There's a rumor going the rounds that if everything goes good in Festung Europa, the war department may cut our term sentence over here from two years to 18 months."

Festung Eupropa was a term used by both sides of the war. For Germany, it meant fortifying the whole of occupied Europe in order to prevent an Allied invasion from the British Isles. For the Allies, it was used in regard to bombing missions by the Royal Air Force on installations in Germany, Italy, and occupied Europe.

JULY 29, 1944

"There seems to be signs of the Germans and Japs starting to crack a bit."

It was only nine days earlier, on July 20, that Hitler survived an assassination attempt by a member of his own inner circle. Colonel Claus Von Stauffenberg orchestrated the unsuccessful attempt on Hiltler's life and was subsequently executed with many other senior officers. The colonel had placed a briefcase with timed explosives beneath a table in Hitler's conference room and then left to await the explosion. Convinced that Hitler had been killed, Stauffenberg flew to Berlin to organize a coup against the Nazi leaders, only to find Hitler was still alive.

Hitler ordered the arrest of over 5,000 people and tortured most of them to learn who had betrayed him. Almost 200 of the people were executed and many more were sent to concentration camps.

On July 21, the United States army retook the island of Guam which was originally captured by the Japanese in

1941. The Americans landing took place on both sides of the Orote Peninsula early in the morning. By nightfall they had established beachheads and began moving inland to take the island. The Japanese waged a fierce fight but by the start of August they were running out of food and supplies. As in other battles in the Pacific, the Japanese refused to surrender and fought until the last soldier was killed.

On August 10, three weeks of bloody fighting after the landing, Guam was declared secure.

"McNair was killed in France and 2 weeks later her only son was killed in Guam. It sure is tough but it's happening every day to someone."

General Lesley James McNair was an American officer who served during World War One and World War Two. He was killed by friendly fire when an air force bomb landed in his foxhole during the battle of Normandy. His son, Colonel Douglas McNair, was chief of staff of the 77th Infantry and was killed two weeks later by sniper fire while serving in Guam.

"The Fighting Sullivans", originally released as "The Sullivans", is a 1944 film which follows the lives of the four Irish-American Sullivan brothers who grew up in Iowa during the Great Depression and served together in the United States Navy during World War Two. Their eventual deaths aboard the USS Juneau (sunk on November 13, 1942 during the Battle of Guadalcanal) were told in the film.

The brothers enlisted in the navy on January 3, 1942 with the stipulation that they serve together. Despite having a policy of not allowing siblings to serve together, the brothers were assigned to the USS Juneau. The Juneau had been hit by a Japanese torpedo early in the Battle of Guadalcanal and was forced to withdraw from the fight. Later in the day, it was struck by a second torpedo, this one striking the ammunition magazines and quickly sank. The USS Helena was in the area, and Captain Gilbert Hoover, skeptical that anyone could have survived the sinking, believed it reckless to look for survivors and risk his already damaged ship to further attack. Instead, Captain Hoover signaled a nearby B-17 to notify Allied headquarters to send aircraft and ships to search for survivors. However, the B-17 was under orders not to break radio silence and did not relate the message regarding searching for survivors until hours later. The B-17 crew's report was mixed with other pending paperwork and not discovered for several days.

Meanwhile, approximately 100 of the Juneau's crew had survived and were left in the water many of whom were seriously wounded. They were exposed to the elements, hunger, thirst, and repeated shark attacks. Eight days after the sinking, ten survivors were found and retrieved from the water. The survivors reported that three of the brothers died instantly, one drowned the next day, and the last survived for five days before suffering from delirium and throwing himself into the water from the raft he occupied.

The navy did not allow the loss of the Juneau to be reported to be sure no information would be available to the enemy. When letters from the sons stopped arriving home, the parents of the Sullivans began to worry. The parents were notified on January 12, 1943 when men in uniform approached the front door and informed Mr. Sullivan, "I have some news for you about your boys." When asked "which one?" the reply was "I'm sorry, all five."

Interestingly, many people thought the movie "Saving Private Ryan" was based on this real life event. However, it was actually based on the Littleton family from the Civil War who lost six sons.

AUGUST 31, 1944

"I probably never mentioned this before, but Gene Markey, husband of Hedy Lamarr has his office a few doors down from ours."

Gene Markey was the second of six husbands for Hedy Lamarr and their marriage lasted from 1939 until 1941. The longest any of Lamarr's marriages lasted was 7 years. She was so unhappy in her first marriage to Friedrich Mandl that she hid from him in a brothel and had sex with a stranger to remain hidden. Later, she hired a maid that looked like her, drugged her, and used the maid's uniform to escape the estate. Lamarr was once considered the "most beautiful woman in Europe" and was very comfortable becoming the first woman to have full frontal nudity in a film.

SEPTEMBER 17, 1944

"I don't know where you got the idea that I said Germany would be beaten this year. I still stick with it that it will be Germany after the first of the year and Japan in the summer of 1946."

117

"A couple of items that I would like for Christmas is a small knife that I can carry with me to use in censoring mail and also a copy of Bob Hope's book "I Never Left Home."

Bob Hope was an English born American comedian, vaudevillian, movie actor, singer, dancer, and author. He appeared on Broadway, in movies, television, and on radio. He made 57 tours for the USO between 1942 and 1988 and became the "first and only honorary veteran of the U.S. Armed Forces" in 1996.

Hope performed his first USO show on May 6, 1941 and continued to perform for U.S. troops regardless of the location, the politics, or the inability to convince other performers to join him. During the Viet Nam war, the anti-war sentiment was so high that Hope became the target of criticism. Some of his shows were drowned out by booing from the crowd and many people considered him an enabler of the war.

Perhaps Bob Hope should be remembered by the words of writer John Steinbeck who was serving as a war correspondent during World War Two. Said Steinbeck of Hope,

"When the time for recognition of service to the nation in wartime comes to be considered, Bob Hope should be high on the list. This man drives himself and is driven. It is impossible to see how he can do so much, cover so much ground, can work so hard, and can be so effective. He works month after month at a pace that would kill most people."

SEPTEMBER 23, 1944

"I met a couple of Dutch seamen a few days ago just after the allies entered Holland and they sure were celebrating."

Allied forces began the invasion of Holland on September 17 as thousands of paratroopers descended into Holland. The Allies considered the Nazi defenses very poor in Holland and wanted to outflank the Germans and hopefully bring an early end to the war. Over 16,500 soldiers dropped into Holland with an additional 3,500 that utilized glider planes.

SEPTEMBER 28, 1944

"You know hon, it's almost, no it's over a year since I saw you last and with me reading about so many soldiers being two timed by their girlfriends at home, it's bound to start a person wondering. Perhaps it's the lack of mail for the past week that's making me wonder about the whole thing."

OCTOBER 16, 1944

"I've been trying to get me a Khukuri knife for some time and finally managed to buy one from one of the little warriors that is supposed to have accounted for 12 slant eyed men."

The khukuri is a Nepalese knife with an inwardly curved edge and is used as both a tool and a weapon. It is the symbolic weapon of the Nepalese Army and is also used in many traditional rituals among different ethnic groups of Nepal.

"Pat O'Brien and Jinx Falkenburg arrived in town today. Pat was emcee and told a few jokes, sang a few Irish songs, and gave his Knute Rockne act. Jinx sang and joked and looked very beautiful."

Pat O'Brien appeared with James Cagney in nine films and they were lifelong friends. In most of the films, O'Brien played a cop or a priest, however he is best known in the title role of the football coach Knute Rockne. It was in that movie that he gave his inspired speech to "win one for the Gipper" referring to the recently deceased football player portrayed by the young Ronald Reagan.

Eugenia "Jinx" Falkenburg was an actress, expert swimmer, and tennis star. At one time, she was the highest paid model and cover girl in the United States. She married journalist and influential publicist Tex McCrary and the two of them were known as "Tex and Jinx". They pioneered and popularized the talk show format on radio and then on television.

Her modeling career skyrocketed in 1937 when she posed for the cover of "The Amercan Magazine". That cover triggered offers from 60 other publications and she eventually wound up being on the cover of over 200 magazines and in nearly 1,500 advertisements. She was considered one of the most beautiful women of the time and The New Yorker magazine said she "possessed one of the most photogenic faces and frames in the western world." Her biggest break as a model came in 1940 when she was selected to be the first "Miss Rheingold". As the face for its marketing campaign, her image graced countless billboards and was featured in advertisements at every store that sold Rhinegold.

While posing for pictures in Hawaii, Jinx fell through a balcony landing on a table thirty feet below. While recovering at a nearby hospital, she met Al Jolson who was also convalescing there. He convinced her to try Broadway and offered her a role in his show "Hold Onto Your Hat." Though her part was small, Jinx stole the show and soon the "Jinx Falkenburg Fan Club" was formed, the only fan club not devoted to a movie star.

"So you and my mom think I'll be home after 18 months. I wish you were right but how can you think that when there are guys over here with 30 to 34 months in this theater."

Tours of duty during World War Two had no specific length. It was based more on the branch of the military, objectives, or location and varied from a few months to a couple of years. Bomber crews had to complete 25 missions before their tour was over. The more often the missions, the shorter their tour.

"What do you think of this Philippine business? We sort of set the Japs back on their buttocks. You ought to hear the Jap radio broadcast from Tokyo and Singapore. It's really amusing to listen to them. The other night they broadcast that they had dispersed our fleet and successfully defended their homeland. Also, they had destroyed 26 B-29's in the air and 47 on the ground. It's really a joke."

The Philippines campaign of 1944–1945 was the campaign to defeat and expel the Japanese forces from the Philippines. The operation began with landings on October 20, 1944 and continued until the end of the war. American bombers were able to conduct regular raids on the Philippines from aircraft carriers. The Americans were also scoring other victories in the Pacific and were getting closer to the nation of Japan.

The Philippine people were ready and waiting for the invasion. When General MacArthur was evacuated in March of 1942, all of the islands fell to the Japanese. The Japanese army was harsh and conducted many atrocities including pressing most of the people into slave labor. The

Americans were aiding the Filipino resistance groups by parachuting supplies allowing the guerrillas to harass the Japanese and control the jungle.

Fighting continued after the landing until August 15, 1945, the day the Japanese surrendered. However, many of the Japanese units were out of radio contact and it was difficult to convince them that the war had ended. Major Japanese officials, including members of the Imperial Family visited in person to convince the solders that they must surrender by order of the Emperor.

"How has Bitzi made out on her endeavor to go AWOL? Personally I think it's a stinking thing for her to do. She volunteered for that duty and the least she could do would be to stick it out. A deserter is one of the lowest if not the lowest forms of humans. It is punishable by death."

More than 40,000 Americans abandoned their posts in World War Two and nearly 100,000 British soldiers did likewise. While desertion is synonymous with cowardice, there were actually many reasons for leaving one's unit. Some needed a break from the constant strain of fighting, others were tempted by women, and some left their troops in the rear to fight at the front.

During the war, the army rate of desertion was over six percent.

NOVEMBER 9, 1944

"We are getting the election returns but they are very early ones and nothing definite yet. Roosevelt at present has 6,200,000 and Dewey 5,100,000. One of those 6 million is my vote. The British over here are very interested in the results and I believe they would like to see FDR remain in there. Most of them think Dewey would turn out to be an isolationist. Leave it to our good ally to be looking out for themselves."

During this election the country was preoccupied with the war. Despite being in office longer than any other president, Franklin Roosevelt remained popular. Dewey ran a very energetic campaign, but, President Roosevelt was able to prevail. Dewey had to defeat four other men to secure the nomination, including General MacArthur, who was actually considered for the Republican nomination, however, it was thought his chances were limited while commanding the forces in the Pacific.

Although the Democrats could not stop Roosevelt from winning the nomination, his obvious physical decline and rumors of his health problems, led the delegates to choose a running mate of their liking. The party leaders informed Roosevelt that they would fight his current vice president, Henry Wallace from running for re-election. The moderate and popular Harry Truman was agreed upon to be Roosevelt's vice president in the election.

While Dewey blasted the President on mainland issues, the victories in France and the Philippines made Roosevelt unbeatable. Roosevelt led Dewey in all the polls and won an easy victory. Roosevelt won 36 states to Dewey's 12 and won the popular vote by over three million. Roosevelt won the election with a lower percentage of both the electoral and popular vote than he had received in his prior election.

DECEMBER 8, 1944

"The way these Japs are going through China I just don't know what to think about the whole deal. I said before we might not defeat the Japs in 1946 but every day looks like it might be later."

The Battle of Changsha was an invasion of the Chinese province by Japanese troops. This was an attempt to establish a land and rail corridor through the Japanese controlled territories.

"Another of my pals got a letter today telling him his girlfriend got married but she still wanted to be friends."

JANUARY 11, 1945

"The night we get married we'll take off for some nice quiet secluded room in some hotel in some city. Then we'll have something to eat and a few drinks after which we will retire by mutual consent to our rendezvous. I can see myself after the rendezvous is over lying very comfortably on a nice soft bed with a dim light on. Then will come the moment I have been waiting for. I'll reach over and get a good 50 cent cigar, light it up and lay back and relax."

JANUARY 12, 1945

"We were discussing the Ohio – Michigan game and I happened to mention that you were there for the game."

At the time the game was played, Michigan was ranked number eight in the country while Ohio State was ranked number seven. Michigan won 7-3.

JANUARY 16, 1945

"I am planning on going to 885 for a few days to settle a few details. I understand it's fairly cold up there dropping to around 35 at night."

JANUARY 18, 1945

"The promotion I've been working so hard for finally came through. It's effective the 5th of January so I found out about it when I het Delhi and had to buy plenty of drinks."

Marvin was promoted to Second Lieutenant.

"Something else I did after 16 months overseas was to finally get a Zippo lighter. The PX received 24 and about 75 signed up to buy one. My number happened to be drawn and I purchased one."

George Blaisdell founded Zippo manufacturing in 1932 and produced the first lighter in 1933. It was inspired by an Austrian lighter of similar design and got its name because Blaisdell liked the sound of the word "zipper". Zippo lighters became so popular in the military that the company ceased producing the lighter for civilians during World War Two. The lighter was originally made of brass but was switched to steel due to the shortage of brass during the war. Despite not having a contract with the armed forces for the PX stores to sell the lighter, military personnel insisted on it being sold.

JANUARY 26, 1945

"Lily Pons is here now with the U.S.O. show and I hope to see her before long."

Lily Pons was a French born operatic soprano and actress who had an active career performing nearly 300 times between 1931 and 1960. In 1944, Pons canceled her fall and winter season in New York and toured with the U.S.O. Her husband was conductor Andre Kostelanetz who directed a band composed of American soldiers. The two performed at military bases in North Africa, Italy, India, and Burma. In 1945, her tour of military bases continued through China, Belgium, France, and Germany before returning home to record breaking crowds at her performances.

In addition to being an opera star, she also had a lucrative and successful career as a concert singer. She made numerous appearances on television and in 1955 she topped the bill for the first broadcast of what became and iconic television series, "Sunday Night at the London Palladium".

Pons was savvy at making herself marketable and her opinions on home decorating and fashion where frequently reported in women's magazines. She was so popular, a town in Maryland named itself after her.

JANUARY 31, 1945

"The war news looks very good in Europe doesn't it? I think it will be over by May and then we finish off Japan next year."

The good news in Europe was the outcome of the Battle of the Bulge. The battle began on December 16, 1944 with the German offensive. By January 25 the German operations had ceased. The Battle of the Bulge was the largest battle fought by the Americans in World War Two. The American troops numbered over 600,000 of which

81,000 of those were lost. The Germans had nearly 100,000 killed, wounded, or captured.

The German goal was to split the Allies line in half, encircle the enemy (destroying four armies in the process), and forcing the Allies to negotiate peace. Then Hitler could focus on the Eastern Front and Russia. The Germans experienced great success at the beginning of the battle. The allies were surprised by the attack due to the lack of any intelligence that the attack had been planned. The Germans had English speaking soldiers dressed in American uniforms causing havoc by spreading misinformation, cutting telephone lines, and changing road signs. Lastly, the weather favored the Germans as it did not allow the superior air forces of the allies to be utilized.

Hitler believed the American forces were incapable of fighting effectively and a decisive defeat would cause the American public's support of the war to wane. He was also hoping that the disputes between British General Montgomery and General Patton would cause confusion among the Allies as they planned a retaliation.

However, the Germans were unable to sustain the fight as it wasn't able to resupply the fuel required to keep the army advancing. In addition, the weather which hampered the Allied air force, also slowed the German advance. When the weather improved, the Allied air force began pummeling the German forces. First, there were air raids on the German supply points and then they began attacking the German troops on the roads.

At the end, the last of the German reserves were destroyed and the Allies were in control of the same areas as before the siege. It was truly the turning point of the war in Europe and began the defeat of Germany.

FEBRUARY 15, 1945

"Hot dog. Good news, good old "der Bingle" is singing "San Fernando Valley" at the present time. I could listen to him all night."

The nickname "Der Bingle" was common among Bing Crosby's German listeners and came to be used by his English speaking fans as well. Crosby made numerous live appearances before American troops fighting in the European Theater. He also learned to pronounce German from written scripts and would read propaganda broadcasts to the German forces. In a poll of U.S. troops at the close of World War Two, Crosby topped the list of people who had done the most for G.I. morale beating out President Roosevelt, General Eisenhower, and Bob Hope.

FEBRUARY 19, 1945

"That's too bad darn bad about Rudy Hagen. War certainly isn't a game by any means but too many people back in the U.S. still think it is. If these politicians would stick to their lobbying and let the conducting of the war to the army, things would be a lot better all around".

Rudy Hagen was a family friend of Marvin's. It illustrates how close to home the tragedies of the war could sometimes become.

MARCH 12, 1945

"For the past couple of weeks our movies have been really terrible. The last one was Judy Canova in "Louisiana Hayride" and we had to fumigate the camp area after they finished showing the film."

MARCH 15, 1945

"My company and I made a trip to Bombay last week and invited the military police to take us on a tour of the brothel section as it's out of bounds to all military personnel. They have one place called the "cage" district which is one long street with rows of houses bordering the street on both sides. It looks like a continuous building as there are no doors in the front only a window and this has bars in it like a cage. The room inside is only about 8 feet square and these girls ranging from 12 years to 60 are locked in these rooms. Customers pick out their choice through the barred window. The girls are usually daughters or wives of men who have become indebted to the owners of these *joints and they stay there until they have worked off the debt. At 2, 4, 6 annas a throw (4, 8, and 12 cents) it usually takes a while."*

There were an estimated 40,000 women working as prostitutes in the brothel district of Bombay during World War Two. The army had Military Police patrolling the area to keep soldiers out, however, the men would resort to any means to employ one of the women. They would even sometimes rent a "gharry", an enclosed horse drawn carriage despite how small it was. The price for the most inexperienced girl was 10 rupees ($3.00) and ranged up to 30 rupees for the best in the brothel.

MARCH 19, 1945

"We've a Japanese news commentator on the air now speaking from Saigon, Indo-China. According to him, we lost an air craft carrier, cruiser, and other assorted vessels yesterday plus 50 or 60 B-29's being shot down. Now they are addressing the Indian people against the British "monster" and saying that India never had anything to fear from the peace loving gentle Japanese. I just wonder how stupid they think we really are but they never give up trying."

Throughout the war, both the Allies and the Axis attempted to sway the opinions of the Indian civilians. The Japanese regarded India as a potential part of their future domain and planned from the outset of the war to subvert the Indian troops. The Japanese distributed leaflets to the Indian border troops asking them to join the Japanese and help liberate India. A "Free India" radio station was created encouraging Indians to rise against the British.

"I received a little shock when I read in the Detroit paper where my former C.O. of C Battery, 82 F.A. was killed in action by a sniper. He was one of the best darn officers that I've ever met and it sure made me feel bad to read that. He recommended me for and helped me go to O.C.S. and I thought a hell of a lot of him. Thirty years old and now look. This war sure is hell and in more ways than one."

"The papers over here seem to be very optimistic about the war in Europe. They say the next 48 hours will be the crisis. Anytime at all now will suit me and a few million others just fine."

The reason for the optimism regarding the end of hostilities in Europe was from General Eisenhower's declaration to the German army and citizenry to surrender. The general summed up his thoughts and feelings in the following letter to President Roosevelt:

Dear Mr. President:

The further this campaign progresses, the more probable it appears that there will never be a clean cut military surrender of forces on the Western Front. Our experience to date is that even when formations as small as a division are disrupted their fragments continue to fight until surrounded. This attitude, if continued, will likely mean that a V-E Day will come about only by proclamation on our part rather than by any definite and decisive collapse or surrender of German resistance.

Projecting this idea further, it would mean that eventually all the areas in which fragments of the German army, particularly the paratrooper, Panzer, and SS elements may be located, will have to be taken by application of or the threat of force. This would lead into a form of guerrilla warfare which would require for its suppression a very large number of troops.

Of course, if the Government of Germany or any group that could take over a political control would make a national surrender, then all armed bodies remaining in the field would, in my opinion, no longer be classed as soldiers of a recognized government, but would occupy the status of brigands or pirates. Since, if captured under these conditions, they would not be entitled to protection afforded by the laws of war, it is my conviction that, except for extreme fanatics, they would largely surrender.

But so long as any of the Hitler gang retains a semblance of political power I believe the effort will be to continue resistance not only throughout Germany, but in all of the outlying areas, including the western port areas of France and Denmark and Norway.

To counteract this eventuality our local propaganda stations are constantly pointing out to the Germans that they should not be planting crops for next winter's food instead of fighting. In addition, I am hopeful of launching operations at the proper time that should partially prevent a guerrilla control of any large area, such as the southern mountain bastion.

It is of course, always possible that there might be in Germany a sudden upsurge of popular resentment against the war, which would lead to a much easier pacification than that described above. My opinion is based upon the supposition that our experience to date provides our best basis of future prediction. At best, we should be prepared for the eventuality described.

DWIGHT D. EISENHOWER

The following is a broadcast that was aired for the German population:

"The following order, dated March 31, 1945, is issued at the order of the Supreme Commander, Allied Expeditionary Forces.

The Allied armies have crossed the Rhine and are driving ever more deeply into the very heart of Germany. The German government has ceased to exercise effective control over wide areas. The German High Command has lose effective control over many units, large and small, of the German forces. In these circumstances, in order to avoid further unnecessary bloodshed and sacrifice of human life, the Supreme Commander of the Allied Expeditionary Forces has issued a series of instructions. Here are instructions to members of the Wehrmacht:

Soldiers of the German Wehrmacht! To save yourselves further useless sacrifice and loss of life, this is what you must do:

Units in contact which no longer receive orders from the German command are to cease hostilities.

Surrender of troop units take place by sending an emissary to the nearest Allied command post under the protection of a white flag.   The surrender must take place in an orderly manner and with observance of military discipline.

The following instructions were issued to foreign workers:

Keep away from all targets, factories, railroads, marshaling yards, and bridges.   Refuse to work in or near such danger spots in which no one has the right to compel anyone to work.

When the Allied armies approach, seek out the safest spot you can find.   Keep off the roads, particularly main highroads.

Stay in those refuges until the Allied armies arrive.   Then report to the Allied Military officials.

Many of your comrades in the areas liberated by the victorious Russian armies owe their freedom to the fact that they were able to put into practice the instructions such as we have just given you.

The Supreme Commander knows your urgent and legitimate desire to return home as soon as possible.   By following these instructions, you will speed up your return to your family.

"Yesterday I was confronted with a very disagreeable task. I was chief witness in a court martial case and I really hated to give testimony which would confine a guy for months and have him lose pay. However, some of these guys still don't understand that they are in the army and rules and regulations are made to be obeyed."

There are three types of court-martials; summary, special, and general. A summary court-martial is composed of one commissioned officer and the accused has the right to a civilian attorney. A special court-martial is made up of at least three members and the accused has the right to a military attorney. A general court-martial has a military judge and at least five members and the accused also has the right to a military attorney.

"On Palm Sunday I happened to mention to one of my boys that it would be a good idea to go to church. He said that he was Catholic but he hadn't been to church in quite a while. I little later he came back and said that he thought he would go to confession

before mass. The only thing that worried him was that he had forgotten how to say the "Act of Contrition". I told him I'd help him to recall it so there he was sitting on a chair trying to recite the Act time after time with me giving him hints every once in a while. Made me feel like a priest."

APRIL 10, 1945

"The officers here had another ration issued them of Schenleys whiskey and as I had 3 bottles already on hand, I offered mine to my enlisted men. If I can help them out once in a while by bringing back memories of good home whiskey, I'll do it."

Enlisted men rations never included any sort of alcoholic beverage.

APRIL 13, 1945

"Listening to the news from London and the 9ᵗʰ army is across the Elbe River about 50 miles from Berlin."

The Allied Armies had pushed the German Army to the east bank of the river Elbe. It was apparent that Germany was losing the war and the Germans had sued for peace on their terms. The Allied Commanders were having none of that and demanded unconditional surrender. A meeting was held between the warring factions and a cease fire was initiated. However, the Germans were proving to be difficult and the Allies commenced hostilities.

April 25, 1945 became known as Elbe Day, the day the Soviet and American troops met at the River Elbe. The meeting of these two armies meant that the German forces had effectively been cut in two.

"It certainly was a shock to hear about our C in C's death and we couldn't believe it was so. We were having a little trouble adjusting our teletype at the time the news was released and meanwhile the British had called us on the telephone to offer condolences. We verified it a few minutes later to our sorrow. The camp flag will be flown at half-mast for 30 days and we also had a brief service yesterday morning. Everyone seems to be taking the news pretty hard even the Indian coolies. How they found out is a mystery but they kept saying "Amreekan bura sahib gone, good sahib." Burra sahb means big or great man. Personally I don't think the carrying on of the war operation will be impaired too greatly but at the peace table we may miss the prestige, influence and respect the President had."

The end of the war in Europe was in sight and President Roosevelt's health had noticeably deteriorated. His complexion and physical weakness had raised concerns among family and associates. The President had traveled to Warm Springs, Georgia, to the "Little White House" as it was called. As he sat in the living room signing letters and documents while posing for a portrait, he grabbed his head complaining of sharp pain. The massive cerebral hemorrhage ended in minutes the life of America's longest serving President.

An editorial by the New York Times declared "Men will thank God on their knees a hundred years from now that Franklin Roosevelt was in the White House."

APRIL 19, 1945

"Received news over our teletype this morning that Ernie Pyle had been killed near Okinawa in the Pacific. That's really tough news as he had made a lot of friends among the GI's and was well liked all over. He was up in Delhi when I first hit there and I saw him on many occasions before he left Delhi for Africa and Italy. It's just like I always said though, when your turn comes around there's no use in worrying."

Ernest Pyle was an American journalist who was known for his columns as a roving correspondent especially in World

War Two when he reported from Europe and the Pacific Theaters. His articles wrote from the perspective of the common soldier. This approach gained him popularity and the Pulitzer Prize. In one of his columns he urged that soldiers should get "fight pay" just as airmen were paid "flight pay". Congress passed a law authorizing an additional $10.00 extra per month for combat infantrymen.

As he was preparing to cover the war in the Pacific, the Navy refused to allow Pyle to use the names of sailors in his reporting. Pyle protested and eventually won as the Navy exclusively allowed him to use the names of sailors.

When Pyle died he was traveling in a jeep with Lieutenant Colonel Joseph Coolidge and three other men. Japanese troops began firing at the jeep and the men jumped into a nearby ditch. Pyle raised his head to check on the others and asked the Colonel "Are you alright?" Those were his last words.

The Ernie Pyle Memorial marks the place where he died. His remains were buried at the Army cemetery on Okinawa and later reinterred at the National Memorial Cemetery of the Pacific in Honolulu. Pyle was one of few

American civilians killed during World War Two to be awarded the Purple Heart.

MAY 7, 1945

"I took time out to get a coke. The army has their own bottling plant here so cokes are rather plentiful."

The president of Coca Cola stood behind his promise that every U.S. serviceperson should be able to get a coke for only five cents no matter where he or she was. This meant sending portable Coca Cola plants around the world to serve over 5 billion bottles during the war.

General Dwight Eisenhower actually requisitioned ten Coca Cola bottling plants for U.S. troops overseas. The telegram sent on June 29, 1943 requested 3 million bottles of Coca Cola and the equipment necessary to make and bottle. All of which had to be shipped without displacing any military cargo.

MAY 10, 1945

"Well I suppose everyone back there is raising the roofs in celebrating the end of the war in Europe. However that's only half of it and we still have a long way to go. I don't know now when I'll be able to go home as the rotation plan is no more."

Victory in Europe Day, known as V E Day, marks the date when the Allies formally accepted the unconditional surrender of Nazi Germany. Since Hitler had committed suicide, the surrender was authorized by his successor Karl Donitz.

The victory happened on President Truman's birthday and he dedicated the moment to his predecessor, Franklin Roosevelt. Despite the triumph, flags remained at half-mast for respect of President Roosevelt.

People in Europe waited patiently for the anticipated announcement regarding the end of the war. By the afternoon, there was still no announcement and bell ringers had been put on standby. Ironically, the Germans had been told by their government that the war was officially over. Joseph Stalin was causing the delay of the allied announcement. Finally, Churchill decided he was not going to allow Stalin the satisfaction of delaying what everyone knew anyway and made the following announcement:

"In accordance with arrangements between the three great powers, tomorrow, Tuesday, will be treated as Victory in Europe Day and will be regarded as a holiday."

The British government also made the following announcement in regards to celebrating:

"Bonfires will be allowed, but the government trusts that only material with no salvage value will be used."

Buckingham Palace was lit up by floodlights for the first time since 1939 and two searchlights made a giant "V" above St. Paul's Cathedral. It was a highly symbolic gesture for a city that had spent years in a blackout.

MAY 22, 1945

"We are living in bamboo huts here at my new location and conditions aren't the best but could be a lot worse. However, don't worry any as I'm quite a way from the Japs and they are leaving Burma (but fast) and not because they want to either."

MAY 26, 1945

"I wrote to Greta last night and told her about the head hunters we have around here. I haven't seen any of the women yet but the guys say they have figures like nobody's business and wear nothing but loin clothes. After seeing how fierce the men appear, I'll keep my distance."

JUNE 14, 1945

"I ran across one of these Naga head hunters the other day while he was washing himself in a pool of water. He looked up at me with a big toothless smile and it was a good thing because if he had scowled I'd have burned a path through that jungle."

The Naga tribe, whose domain straddles the Burma-China border, were once known as the Wild Wa" for their savage behavior.

JUNE 18, 1945

"I noticed in our news report that we get daily on our teletype a little notice that I remember all too well. Perhaps you'll recall some time ago that I told you to remember a certain date namely November 26, 1943. Well, in this article you'll understand why as the ship I was on was within throwing distance of the Rhona. A hot time was had by all but it certainly was a sickening sight to behold and one I'll probably never forget."

JUNE 22, 1945

"We are really losing a lot of generals over here as 2 were killed on Okinawa this week alone. That island is proving very costly but it well prove very valuable for future operations."

On June 18, 1945, with victory imminent, General Buckner, the hero of Iwo Jima, was killed by Japanese artillery. Three days later, his 10th army reached the southern coast of the island, and on June 22 Japanese resistance effectively came to an end.

156

The Japanese lost 120,000 troops in the defense of Okinawa, while the Americans suffered 12,500 dead and 35,000 wounded. Of the 36 Allied ships lost, most were destroyed by the over 2,000 Japanese pilots who gave up their lives in kamikaze missions. With the capture of Okinawa, the Allies prepared for the invasion of Japan, a military operation predicted to be far bloodier than D Day. The plan called for invading the southern island of Kyoshu in November of 1945 and the main Japanese island of Honshu in March of 1946.

JUNE 26, 1945

"We got our jungle ration which consisted of one bottle of scotch. I've found out that there's nothing to compare with good scotch and a little water. I almost had heart failure that day I came down here. I was at the air strip waiting for someone to come and get me when some jerk ran over my briefcase with a jeep. The bad part about it was that I had 3 radio tubes, one quart of scotch, and some cigars it it. The cigars were ok, but 2 of the tubes were broken. The scotch which I have been saving for 6 months was un damaged (sigh of relief)."

JULY 2, 1945

"My mail has been coming in terribly since I've been here. Our mail has to be flown in and I guess they don't make it sometimes. The weather is very bad for flying and the terrain is just as risky. About 5 P.M. I noticed large billows of black smoke rising a few miles away so I imagine another went down."

JULY 7, 1945

"It used to get hot in Delhi (around 140) but it was a dry heat and a person didn't perspire, he just roasted slowly. Right now it's around 9 P.M. and I'm sitting here with a bath towel underneath my shirt collar to absorb the dampness. We are required to wear long sleeves after 6 P.M. as a malaria prevention measure. I haven't turned yellow yet from the atabrine but I may eventually."

India during the summer can have temperatures as high as 120 degrees but will feel warmer due to the very hot and dry winds. The extreme heat is also due to the constant sun and low humidity.

JULY 14, 1945

"As far as worrying about me there's very little danger near here as the Japs are about 300 miles from here. They are still raising a little hell in lower Burma but nothing much to bother us any."

159

JULY 23, 1945

"I came down her to Bhamo yesterday afternoon and plan on going back to Myitkyana in the morning. This place is almost a complete wreck. There are shell holes and bomb craters all over the place even on the roads and haven't been filled yet. There are also hundreds of Japanese dugouts with tunnels leading from one to another like a bunch of rats. They really went to a lot of labor to defend this place."

The market town of Bhamo, located on the navigable Ayeyarwady River, had been built up by the Japanese as a defensive fortress since the beginning of 1944. The area was divided into three fortress areas that stood at high grounds. Starting in November of 1944 elements of the 38th Division was able to eliminate Japanese bunkers one by one, but their success brought alarm to the Japanese command, who reinforced Bhamo by sending Colonel Yamazaki's 3,000 man force. Yamazaki's men, however, were unable to make it to Bhamo and it soon fell to the Chinese. This allowed the Allies to finally utilize the infamous Burma Road, a supply lane to China.

"The other place that was interesting was a small fort in the center of town. Some of the Japs made a last ditch stand there and it took quite a lot of shelling before they surrendered. The place is now surrounded by barbed wire 30 feet high and inside as prisoners are kept Japanese Geisha girls and "comfort" girls that accompanied the troops. Rather a practical idea these Japs had, don't you think? Just like a ration, one girl to every 10 men."

Comfort women were women and girls who worked either voluntarily or involuntarily in a prostitution corps created by the Empire of Japan. The Japanese Army was involved with the coercing, deceiving, luring, and sometimes kidnapping of young women throughout Japan's occupied territories. The number of women involved range from 20,000 to as high as 410,000.

According to reports, young women from countries under Japanese control were abducted from their homes or lured with promises of work in factories or restaurants. Once recruited, the women were incarcerated into "comfort stations".

Some in the Japanese command felt that by providing comfort women it would reduce the number of rape crimes committed by the Japanese Army and thus prevented the rise of hostility among the people in the occupied areas. It also was thought to help prevent the spread of venereal disease and control the simmering discontentment among the Japanese soldiers.

The Allied forces captured "comfort women" as well as Japanese soldiers and issued reports on them. An Army interrogator reported that "comfort women" were nothing more than prostitutes attached to the Japanese Army. They lived well because their food and material was not rationed and they were paid handsomely.

"If you want to do me a favor, please don't ask me in your letters about how many points I have or if I've found out anything new. Frankly I expect to be very, very lucky to get home this year at all. At the present time, it looks very black and I'm not being pessimistic but revealing what I expect. If something happens to bring me home earlier then I won't complain a bit."

Soldiers earned points according to the number of months in the army (1 point per month), number of months overseas (1 point per month), number of months in a combat zone (3 points per month), number of wounds received (6 points per Purple Heart), and number of dependent children under 18 (12 points per child). Each rank had its own required points for discharge. Colonels through Majors needed 100 points, Captains through Lieutenants needed 85 points, and enlisted required 60 points.

"We got our monthly ration of whiskey yesterday but I think that next month's will be the last. The reason they are stopping it is that too many enlisted men were writing into Yank Magazine complaining about officers getting it but they couldn't. These GI's are always bitching about something or other. They hate to see an officer have anything that they can't yet they all started out in the army on an equal basis with us. The reason they aren't officers is that they are damn lazy, lack initiative, or intelligence."

"I see by the news today that Japan rejected our proposals for their surrender. Personally I wasn't foolish enough to think they would accept it simple because of the fanatical defense they have put up everywhere we have met them. General Sultan, who led out troops over here in Burma, says that we won't defeat them for at least a year and perhaps 2 years. I agree with him but I stick to my original "guess" of August or September 1946. I sincerely hope that I won't be here at that date."

It was decided to issue a statement, the Potsdam Declaration, defining "Unconditional Surrender" and clarifying what it meant for the position of the emperor and for Hirohito personally. The American and British governments strongly disagreed on this point, the United States wanted to try him as a war criminal, while the British simply wanted Hirohito to resign. On July 26, the United States, Britain, and China released the Potsdam Declaration announcing the terms for Japan's surrender with the warning "We will not deviate from them. There are no alternatives. We shall brook no delay."

The Declaration ended with the following:

"We call upon the government of Japan to proclaim now the unconditional surrender of all Japanese armed forces, and to provide proper and adequate assurances of their good faith in such action. The alternative for Japan is prompt and utter destruction."

The "prompt and utter destruction" clause is a veiled warning about the American possession of the atomic bomb.

The Japanese government debated how to respond to the declaration. It was decided not to respond until it could get more information from the Soviets who had signed a neutrality pact with Japan prior to the war. The Japanese decided to reject the surrender offer stating:

"The only thing to do is just kill it with silence (mokusatsu). We will do nothing but press on to the bitter end to bring about a successful completion of the war." The term "mokusatsu" literally means "kill with silence" and can range from ignore to treat with contempt.

AUGUST 8, 1945

"I found a large leech on the floor of my tent yesterday and had quite a time evicting him. I've seen a lot of scars left by these leeches on the legs of some of the enlisted men who work in the swamps and jungles."

Leeches attach themselves when they bite and will stay attached until it becomes full and then falls off to digest. Due to its secretions, the bites bleed more than a normal wound once the leech is removed.

"According to my records I don't believe I've written a letter since last Sunday. This is due to various reasons but mainly to a 3 day celebration during which I and practically every person in the company got plastered. The war is over, thank God, but not completely. A lot of Japs have been cut off in lower Burma and don't know the Japs have surrendered. The Japs seem to be stalling right now so I'm in favor of dropping a few more atomic bombs on them to speed them up a little. Boy, would I love to be marching into Tokyo."

AUGUST 24, 1945

"As far as that bet is concerned between my brother Clayt and my mom, I think Clayt has the better chance to win. The news is on now and the Japs are supposed to surrender on August 31 in Tokyo Bay. If V J day is declared officially September 2, I'll win a pool of 150 rupees or approximately 48 dollars."

Victory over Japan Day, also known as V J day, is the term applied to both August 14 and August 15 due to the time zone differences. It also is considered to be September 2, which is the day of the signing of the surrender document on the USS Missouri.

On August 6 and August 9 the United States dropped atomic bombs on Hiroshima and Nagasaki. In addition, the Soviet Union officially declared war on Japan on August 9. The government of Japan communicated its intention to surrender on August 10, but there were too many conditions and it was rejected by the Allies. The news of the Japanese offer touched off celebrations around the world. Germany stated that the Japanese were wise enough, unlike themselves, to give up in a hopeless situation and were grateful the atomic bomb was not ready in time to be used on them.

Finally, shortly after noon on August 15, Japan announced it was accepting the terms of surrender outlined in the Potsdam Declaration. The Japanese Navy was no longer capable of conducting operations and an Allied invasion of Japan was imminent. While Japan was publicly posturing to fight until the bitter end, it was privately making entreaties to the Soviet Union to negotiate a peace favorable to the Japanese. Little did the Japanese realize, but the Soviets were about to break the Soviet-Japanese Neutrality Pact and were preparing to attack Japan.

The Japanese fleet was virtually destroyed and Japan had very little natural resources or raw materials remaining. The Japanese industry had been wrecked by the Allied bombing leaving the Imperial Headquarters to conclude the following:

"We can no longer direct the war with any hope of success. The only course left is for Japan's one hundred million people to sacrifice their lives by charging the enemy to make them lose the will to fight."

The Japanese government had planned an all-out defense of Kyushu codenamed Operation Ketsugo. In it, everything was staked on the beachhead and more than 3,000 kamikazes would be sent to attack the amphibious transports to stop the Allied troops from landing. If this did not work, they planned to send an additional 3,500 kamikazes and 5,000 shin yo suicide boats to stop the assault.

All of this preparation and planning had actually begun back in June for the Japanese emperor. When Japan lost the Battle of Okinawa, and he learned the weakness of the Japanese army in China, and the devastation of the Japanese fleet, he concluded he could no longer defend the Home Islands. He also learned that there weren't enough weapons to arm the soldiers of Japan. The Emperor stated:

"I was told that iron from bomb fragments dropped by the enemy was being used to make shovels. This confirmed my opinion that we were no longer in a position to continue the war".

As Japan utilized its diplomatic connections with the Soviet Union and Switzerland to attempt to orchestrate a surrender on its terms, American cryptographers had broken nearly all of Japan's codes, including the Purple Code used by the Japanese foreign office. As a result, messages between Japan's embassies were provided to Allied policy makers nearly as quickly as to the intended recipients.

When the first atomic bomb was dropped on Hiroshima, confused reports reached Tokyo that Hiroshima had been leveled with a "blinding flash and violent blast". Later in the day, President Truman announced the use of the atomic bomb stating:

"We are now prepared to obliterate more rapidly and completely every productive enterprise the Japanese have above the ground in any city. We shall destroy their docks, their factories, and their communication. Let there be no mistake, we shall completely destroy Japan's power to make war. It was to spare the Japanese people from utter destruction that the ultimatum of July 26 was issued at Postdam. Their leaders promptly rejected that ultimatum. If they do not accept our terms they may expect a rain of ruin from the air, the like of which has never been seen on this earth".

SEPTEMBER 1, 1945

"I found a picture of me that I had taken in the jungle about a year ago for an identification card. I appear a little worse for wear and tear but still alive and kicking which is a lot more than a million or so other guys."

"Nothing definite around here as to what's going to happen about our going home. All kinds of rumors but no one knows anything yet. I have very high hopes of being home for Christmas and can't see very many if any reason why I shouldn't."

SEPTEMBER 5, 1945

"In the news this morning I noticed where there are thousands on strike in Detroit over the grievances they put up with during the war. What a country and so many stupid people."

Walter Reuther led the UAW to strike, not because of wartime grievances, but because Reuther feared the power of the corporation. Reuther claimed that the controllers of technology in the auto industry used their power to maximize profits by pursuing a program of planned scarcity which would drive up prices and cut jobs. Reuther went on to claim "there can be no permanent prosperity as long as the controls of production remain in the hands of the privileged few."

Reuther demanded a thirty percent increase in hourly wages and a halt on car prices. When General Motors rejected his offer, Reuther demanded that General Motors open their books to prove they couldn't afford the wage increase and cap on car prices. This time, General Motors declared Reuther to be un-American and a socialist.

The strike was settled in March of 1946 as the UAW accepted a raise of 17.5 percent.

SEPTEMBER 6, 1945

"They announced today that officers would need 85 points and up to get released from the army. At the present time I have around 78 so that keeps me in. However, if an officer is declared surplus or has no suitable assignment he can be discharged without regard to the number of points he has. I'm still hoping to get home this year but one day it looks good and the next day very bad."

"In just three more weeks I'll have completed two years overseas. That's one hell of a long time. Some of the things I've seen I don't like to try to recall. I'll probably never forget how I was praying, holding my breath, sweating, almost ruined my trousers while watching a whole string of bombs descend on our ship."

SEPTEMBER 14, 1945

"I found out today that I've been put in for another combat star and that will make my point score up to VJ Day a total of 81."

174

SEPTEMBER 22, 1945

"We have a coke bottling plant set up here now and we get one bottle per day. Just think of that, one per day. Boy is this place getting civilized."

SEPTEMBER 29, 1945

"I am back in Ledo as one of the officers had enough points to go home so I came up here to take over his job until I go home. Right now I am in charge of all radio and teletype for all of Burma up to the China border."

OCTOBER 4, 1945

"As of 10 P.M. which is now, we are supposed to leave here with the 31st signal battalion for Chabrea to Karachi to board ship for the states."

OCTOBER 11, 1945

"Well, I'm one more step nearer home as we got here in Kauachi the night before last. We left Chabua at 8:30 A.M. in a C-54 Skymaster, which is one of those large 4 engine cargo planes. We made the non stop trip on 1700 miles in 9 ½ hours."

OCTOBER 29, 1945

"You seemed fairly certain that I was on my way home because you hadn't heard from me. The fact of the matter was that a 4 week backlog of mail, amounting to 14 tons was laying at Casablanca. Prisoners and wounded had a higher priority than mail did. Prisoners meaning our liberated prisoners. We should pull into New York harbor around the 20ᵗʰ of November so it looks like I'll miss Thanksgiving at home by a few days."

NOVEMBER 6, 1945

"The only bad feature of this trip is that there are 65 WAC's aboard and so we can't take our sun baths. The WAC's seem very well behaved and don't at all justify or merit the name that people back home have given them."

Marvin Lazette was honorably discharged from the army in September of 1945. He had ascended from private to the rank of second lieutenant during the one year enlistment that lasted over four years. He returned home to Monroe where he married his girlfriend and war time pen pal Bertha Balk, and went back to work at the Woodall factory. He raised a son and a daughter.

While he didn't make the ultimate sacrifice for his country, he did give over four years of his life in conditions that were always rigorous and sometimes dangerous. He saw the horrors of war while witnessing the bombing and ultimate sinking of a troop ship and endured life away from home and loved ones. His story, thoughts, and feelings are probably echoed by the thousands of soldiers who served our country during World War Two. To him and them, I express my thanks and gratitude, and hope this book helps bring their story and trials to the many who only think they understand the meaning of sacrifice.

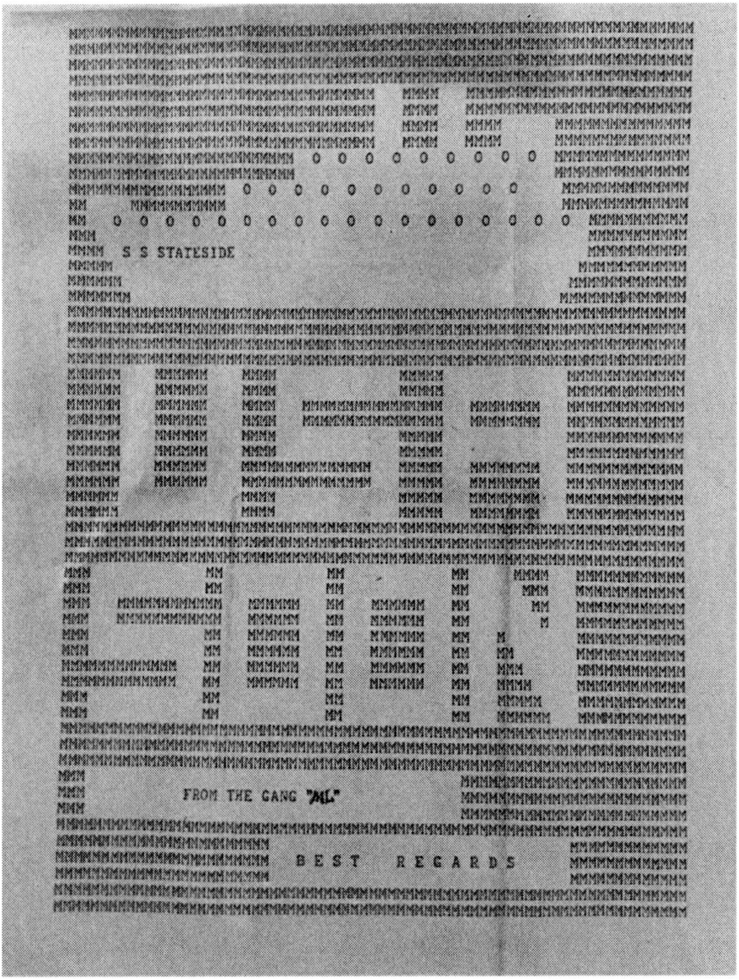
S S STATESIDE
FROM THE GANG "ML"
B E S T R E G A R D S